ADVANCES IN THE FORENSIC ANALYSIS AND DATING OF WRITING INK

ABOUT THE AUTHORS

Richard L. Brunelle has a bachelor's degree majoring in chemistry obtained from Clark University in Worcester, Massachusetts and a masters of science degree majoring in Forensic Science obtained from The George Washington University in Washington, DC. Most of his career was spent with the Bureau of Alcohol, Tobacco and Firearms (ATF), where he retired in 1988 as Chief of their Forensic Science Laboratory with 28 years of government service. After retirement from ATF, he established and operated Brunelle Forensic Laboratories for ten years, where he specialized in the dating of inks on questioned documents.

During his career, Brunelle published approximately 50 scientific publications, including a textbook on the Forensic Examination of Ink and Paper, a chapter in a Handbook of Forensic Sciences, and a chapter in an Encyclopedia of Forensic Sciences. He was the recipient of the John A. Dondero Memorial Award, presented to him by the International Association for Identification for developing the first capability in the United States for dating inks. He also established the Society of Forensic Ink Analysts (SOFIA), which was incorporated in Virginia in 1997. This was the first professional association in the world for forensic ink chemists.

Kenneth R. Crawford received a Bachelor of Arts in Biology and a Bachelor of Science in Zoology from the University of Texas at Austin. He served as a Forensic Document Examiner and Ink Analyst for the Texas Department of Public Safety Crime Laboratory for over 25 years.

ADVANCES IN THE FORENSIC ANALYSIS AND DATING OF WRITING INK

By

RICHARD L. BRUNELLE, M.S.

and

KENNETH R. CRAWFORD, B.A., B.S.

CHARLES C THOMAS · PUBLISHER, LTD.
Springfield · Illinois · U.S.A.

Published and Distributed Throughout the World by

CHARLES C THOMAS • PUBLISHER, LTD.
2600 South First Street
Springfield, Illinois 62704

© 2003 by CHARLES C THOMAS • PUBLISHER, LTD.

ISBN 0-398-07346-5 (hard)
ISBN 0-398-07347-3 (paper)

Library of Congress Catalog Card Number: 2002020460

Printed in the United States of America
MM-R-3

Library of Congress Cataloging-in-Publication Data

Brunelle, Richard L.
    Advances in the forensic analysis and dating of writing ink / by Richard L.
Brunelle and Kenneth R. Crawford.
        p. cm.
    Includes bibliographical references and index.
    ISBN 0-398-07346-5 (hard) -- ISBN 0-398-07347-3 (pbk.)
    1. Writing–Identification. 2. Ink. I. Crawford, Kenneth R. II. Title.

HV8076 .B78 2002
363.25'65–dc21   2002020460

Dedicated
to the Memory of
Dawn Marie

PREFACE

The dating of documents has become a valuable tool for the detection of fraud. Ink dating chemists in the federal government, and in the private sector, routinely conduct examinations of documents submitted in connection with a wide variety of criminal and civil investigations.

The reasons these examinations have become so important is simple–they provide conclusive proof of fraud, when it exists–and a strong case for authenticity, when there is no evidence of fraud. Ink dating techniques have been instrumental in resolving many headline criminal investigations, such as the investigations of former Vice-President Spiro Agnew; the Howard Hughes (Mormon Will); the mass murderer, Juan Corona; and Watergate. The Mussolini and Jack the Ripper diaries were also proven to be frauds by ink dating.

Many civil cases do not make the headlines, but they often involve millions, if not billions of dollars. Ink examinations have been performed on documents in connection with numerous patent disputes, such as the patent for the manufacture of acid and stone washed jeans, the patent for certain video games made by Nintendo and Atari, and the invention of the laproscope. Medical malpractice, altered wills, divorces, wrongful terminations, insurance fraud, sexual harassment, copyrights, labor-management disputes, and legal malpractice are all situations that routinely require the dating of documents. Therefore it should be no surprise that these advances are rapidly becoming known worldwide by forensic chemists, document examiners, and by law firms that routinely question the authenticity of documents.

This book describes in detail the many advances that have occurred in methods used to date inks on questioned documents, since the publication of *Forensic Examination of Ink And Paper* in 1984. Using the methods described in this book, forensic chemists interested in this line of work will be able learn how to compare, identify, and date inks on questioned documents.

Document examiners, who are usually the first to examine a questioned document, will learn the capabilities that exist with respect to ink dating. This will enable them to advise lawyers, when ink dating examinations are appropriate. Lawyers will be better able to conduct direct and cross-examinations of ink dating chemists and university professors will have a useful text to use in their forensic programs.

I would like to take this opportunity thank my wife, Diane, for her love and support and for encouraging me to do something useful in my retirement. She is the one who had to tolerate my moods during the writing of this book. I thank my daughters, Desiree and Holly for their everlasting love and unqualified support of everything I have done in my life. I thank my grandchildren, Jason, Tina, Jake, and Sam, for their love and for adding so much more meaning to my life. My thanks also go to my new family, Jason, Andrea, Tim, and Chris for their love and sincere interest in my accomplishments. The love of Joe, my son-in-law, and Sue, my favorite partner in cards, is equally appreciated.

Tony Cantu provided much appreciated technical advice for this book as he has provided ink analysts for decades. His many published papers are cited as technical references in the following pages. Al Lyter is to be thanked for his contribution of known dated ink samples for some of the experiments first described in this book. In addition, his research is also cited more than once. Robert L. Kuranz and Dr. Ben Fabien are recognized for providing technical review of the chapter on ink chemistry.

Lastly, my sincere thanks go to Erich Speckin who contributed some of the illustrations in this text. More importantly, I thank him for taking up the profession of forensic ink dating, which will help provide longevity to the profession I have loved for over 30 years.

R.L.B.

INTRODUCTION

The forensic examination and dating of documents is important in our society, because documents are used throughout our lives to record everything we do. It starts with our birth certificate and ends with our death certificate. In between birth and death, there are receipts, leases, deeds, contracts, checks, wills, sales agreements, promissory notes, loans, medical records, and yes, even tax returns. The validity of all of these documents is often questioned during litigation. In fact, no other instrument of crime is as prevalent in our society as the document. Newspapers and the media report rapes, murders, bombings, kidnappings, fires, and other violent crimes. Yet, crimes committed with documents involve billions of dollars annually and actually have a bigger impact on society than do violent crimes.

Since the development of the first ink dating capabilities in 1968,[1] there have been many advances in this field. Now, not only can the first date of manufacture of an ink be determined, it is also possible to determine when an ink was written on a document. As a result, federal and local law enforcement agencies are routinely relying on these techniques in their criminal investigations. In civil areas, lawyers call on ink dating specialists in the private sector to date documents involved in a wide variety of cases. Such cases involve medical malpractice, altered wills, patent disputes, divorces, tax fraud, stock fraud, insurance fraud, discrimination, sexual harassment, wrongful terminations, labor-management disputes, copyright cases, and a wide variety of contractual disputes.

Documents may contain several items that can be chemically analyzed for dating purposes. These items include writing inks, paper, correction fluids, photocopy toners, laser printer toners, ink jet printer inks, and typewriter inks. The most useful of these for dating purposes are writing inks.

The Forensic Examination of Ink and Paper,[2] published in 1984 by Charles C Thomas, Publisher, provides a complete description of methods used to analyze and date inks and paper at that time. That text also covers the historical development of writing inks and their chemical properties, manufacturing processes, writing instruments, printing inks, typewriting inks, and paper manufacturing processes. Since this text endeavors not to overlap *The Forensic Examination of Ink and Paper*, readers should be familiar with the contents of that book before reading about the advances described in this text.

This text describes the advances that have occurred since 1984 for the chemical comparison, identification and dating of writing inks, as well as discussion of new writing inks that have been developed. Advances in the dating of inks are primarily in the area of relative age comparisons (ink dryness measurements) and the accelerated aging of inks. These methods involve comparing the relative dryness of questioned inks with known dated inks of the same formulation, stored under the same conditions and written on similar paper. Accelerated aging of inks can be used to date inks, when known dated inks are not available. Both of these methods measure rates or extents of extraction of the inks with weak and strong solvents. Some methods measure only the volatile components of inks.

We have not covered the examination of paper in this text because few advances have occurred in this area. In addition to detailed descriptions of new laboratory techniques, we will present actual case examinations and results. We will discuss Court admissibility of the methods according to the Frye and Daubert rules, as well as the establishment of a new professional association dealing with forensic ink examinations, The Society of Forensic Ink Analysts (SOFIA).

REFERENCES

1. Brunelle, R. L. & Pro, M. J.: A systematic approach to ink identification. JAOAC, 55: 823, 1972.
2. Brunelle, R. L. & Reed, R. W.: Forensic Examination of Ink and Paper. Springfield, IL, Charles C Thomas, 1984.

CONTENTS

ILLUSTRATIONS

TABLES

ADVANCES IN THE FORENSIC ANALYSIS AND DATING OF WRITING INK

Chapter 1

HISTORICAL DEVELOPMENT:
HOW WE GOT HERE

BACKGROUND

To appreciate the current state-of-the-art of the forensic comparison, identification, and dating of inks, it is necessary to acknowledge the pioneering work done by our predecessors in this field.

Their accomplishments have paved the way for the techniques that are in use today. The most significant early work in the comparison of fountain pen inks was Mitchell's *Inks: Their Composition And Manufacture*,[1] published in 1904. Mitchell updated this work in 1937, when he published another book with the same title.[2]

While numerous articles were published on the differentiation of inks, only a few researchers published procedures for dating inks. Witte[3] described the early work of Hess, Mitchell, and others for the dating of fountain pen inks. These studies were done about 1930 and involved the relative aging of inks using ion (chloride and sulfate), migration, fading, and extractability.

Witte developed techniques for removing microdiscs of ink on paper for chemical analysis in 1963. In 1968, Brunelle developed a similar microplug sampling technique. His procedure used a 20-gauge hollow-point needle and syringe to remove ink from documents. These developments were important because, for the first time, chemical tests could be performed on the ink without significant damage to the documents examined.

Research on methods to compare inks rapidly increased, beginning about 1950. Paper chromatography,[4] thin-layer chromatography,[5] electrophoresis,[6] chemical spot tests,[7] gas chromatography,[8] high-performance liquid chromatography,[9] and infrared spectroscopy,[10] were all used for the comparison of inks. Eventually, thin-layer chromatography became the method of choice for comparing inks, because of its simplicity, reliability, and low cost. In the early 1960s, Werner Hofmann with the Zurich Cantonal Police Laboratory, used a standard ink reference collection to identify and to determine the first date of manufacture of ballpoint inks.[11] He used paper chromatography, TLC, spectrophotometry, spot tests, and the usual non-destructive tests to compare and match questioned and known inks.

All of the above accomplishments paved the way for Brunelle to establish the first systematic approach for the identification and dating of inks in the United States in 1968 at the Bureau of Alcohol, Tobacco and Firearms. He compiled a comprehensive Standard Ink Reference Collection, consisting of inks manufactured throughout the world.[12] By comparing the dye compositions of questioned inks with the standard inks, he was able to identify the questioned ink and determine when that ink was first manufactured. This was the beginning of ink dating as it is known today in the United States. This ink reference collection was transferred from ATF to the United States Secret Service Forensic Laboratory upon Brunelle's retirement in 1988. The Standard Ink Reference Collection is the largest in the world and now consists of over seven thousand different formulations of ink.

DATING OF FOUNTAIN PEN INKS

Mitchell's 1937 book describes chemical tests on iron gallotannate inks to estimate their age. These tests were based on the color of blue-black inks and the speed of reaction of the inks with certain chemicals. The color tests required standards of known age. He compared the rate of disappearance of the blue color of questioned inks with the known dated standards. The chemical tests measured the effect of oxalic acid on the pigment iron gallotannate. Mitchell found that the black pigment in freshly written inks bleached immediately and the blue color spread over the paper when the ink was treated with oxalic acid. Older inks, three or four years old, reacted slowly to oxalic acid and the blue color did not diffuse over the paper.

Mitchell was probably the first researcher to experiment with the dryness of fountain pen inks on paper. He theorized that the iron gallotannate first formed is readily soluble in dilute acids. As oxidation proceeds, a resinous tannate is slowly formed until the tannate ink becomes insoluble in the dilute acids.

Kikuchi's research provided the basis for the solvent extraction techniques in use today for estimating the age of writing inks. She reported this work in 1959.[13] Her technique measures the time it takes for blue-black inks to disperse on paper when solvents are applied to the ink on paper. Kikuchi noticed that newer inks dispersed more quickly than older inks.

In 1984, McNeil reported the use of Scanning Auger Microscopy for dating manuscript iron gallotannate inks.[14] His method is limited to historical documents because the accuracy is limited to plus or minus about 22 years. The technique measures the outward migration of iron atoms from the ink boundary along a fibril. The migration increases exponentially with the age of the iron gallotannate ink. The absolute dating of the iron gallotannate inks is possible because the procedure is not affected by temperature or humidity. This means it is not necessary to have standard inks of known age for comparison.

DATING OF BALLPOINT AND NON BALLPOINT INKS

Credit for the development of the first ballpoint pen in 1939 is given to Ladislao Biro. Marketing of this new pen in the United States did not begin until about 1945, when 50,000 pens were sold at Gimbel's Department Store in New York City.

Changes in the chemical composition of ballpoint inks have occurred since their early development. Knowledge of these changes–and when they occurred–can be used for dating purposes. The first ballpoint inks were made with oil-based solvents like mineral oil, linseed oil, and recinoleic acid. Around 1950, ballpoint inks changed from oil base to a glycol base. Oil-base and glycol-base ballpoint inks are readily distinguishable because oil-base inks are soluble in petroleum ether–if the ink has been on paper less than 5 to 10 years. With age, oil-base ink becomes completely insoluble in petroleum ether. Glycol-base inks are insoluble in petroleum ether.

About 1954, another change to the composition of ballpoint inks occurred. Chelated metalized dyes began to be used. The most frequently used of these dyes is the blue-green copper phthalocyanine dye. This class of dyes is stable to light and has excellent solubility properties. A simple solubility test using methanol can determine if an ink contains copper phthalocyanine.

Pentel of Japan introduced a new fiber tip writing instrument in 1962. This pen was followed quickly by plastic nib and other porous tip pens. United States manufacturers began making these pens about 1965. Inks used in these pens are readily distinguishable from fountain pen and ballpoint inks because of their distinctive visual and microscopic appearance and their dye compositions. These inks can be either water-soluble or water resistant.

In 1978, Anja and Papermate simultaneously developed another new ink–the erasable ballpoint ink. This ink has a rubber cement consistency and can be erased if erased within about a day of when the writing occurred. Its visual appearance is not readily distinguishable from other ballpoint inks, but its dye composition is.

The roller ball pen was introduced around 1968. The ink used in these pens is similar to the inks used in porous or fiber tip pens. The dyes are the same and most of them are water base. Writing made with a roller ball pen is similar to the writing of a fountain pen in that fiber diffusion is common.

Striations usually present in the stroke of a ballpoint pen are absent in the writing of a roller ball pen because roller ball inks flow freely over the fibers of the paper, filling in any striations that might otherwise be visible.

Brunelle and Cantu developed an ink-tagging program in 1975 at the Bureau of Alcohol, Tobacco and Firearms. The purpose of this program was to be able to determine the actual year an ink was made by an ink manufacturer. Manufacturers changed the tags annually on a 10-year cycle. Some companies added rare earth chelates, which could be detected by x-ray excited optical emission spectroscopy.

One company added optical whiteners as the tags and these were detected by TLC. This tagging program was very helpful in detecting backdated documents; however, both tagging programs were discontinued when the United States Secret Service assumed responsibility for these programs upon Brunelle's retirement.

The latest type of ink to enter the marketplace is gel-pen ink, which was introduced during the mid 1980s by the Japanese. Four brands of gel-pen inks have been introduced by Japan–the Uniball Signo by Mitsubishi; the Zebra J-5, 3; the Pentel Hybrid; and the Sakura Gelly

Table 1.1
IMPORTANT DATES FOR DATING INKS

Event	Date
India/Carbon Inks	618-906 AD
Iron Gallotannate Inks	about 600 AD
Fountain Pen Inks:	
• Gallotannate	1880s
• Blue Black	1880s
• Modern Washable	1940s
Ballpoint Inks	1939 (in Europe)
• Oil Base	1945 (in the U.S.)
• Glycol Base	1951
• Erasable	1963
• Pressurized	1968
Copper Phthalocyanine Dye	1954
Fiber/ Porous Tip Pen Inks	1962 (in Japan)
	1965 (in the U.S.)
Rolling Ball Marker Inks	1968
Gel-Pen Inks	Mid-1980s (in Japan)
	About 1990 (in the U.S.)

Roll pen. The first known supply of these pens reached the United States about 1993. One United States manufacturer is now producing these inks–National Ink. Gel-pen inks predominately utilize colored pigments rather than organic dyes. Those that contain pigments only are totally insoluble, even in the strongest of organic solvents. The ink is a gel, not a liquid. These chemical properties make it impossible to analyze by traditional methods, when trying to compare the similarity of two or more inks. Therefore, the new relative age comparison tests, based on solvent extraction techniques, will not work on gel-pen inks.

The current state-of-the-art for dating writing inks is based on relative age comparison tests (ink dryness tests) and accelerated aging of inks, developed by Cantu and Brunelle.[15,16,17,18]

These methods, which are based on solvent extraction and changes in dye concentrations, are described in detail in the "Relative Age Comparison Tests" section of Chapter 8.

REFERENCES

1. Mitchell, C. A.: *Inks: Their Composition and Manufacture.* London, Griffin, 1907.
2. Mitchell, C. A.: *Inks: Their Composition and Manufacture.* London, Griffin, 1937.
3. Witte, A. H.: The examination and identification of inks. *Methods of Forensic Science*, 2: F. Lundquist (Ed.), New York, Interscience, 1963.
4. Somerford A. W. & Souder, J. L.: Examination of fluid writing inks by paper chromatography. *J. Crim. Law*, 43: 124, 1952.
5. Thol, J.: Analysis of ballpoint inks by thin-layer chromatography. *Police*, 7: 63, 1960.
6. Brown, C. & Kirk, P. L.: Comparison of writing inks using electrophoresis. *J. Crim. Law*, 45: 334, 1954.
7. Crown, D. A., Conway, J. U. & Kirk, P. L.: Differentiation of blue ballpoint inks using chemical spot tests. *J. Crim. Law*, 52: 338, 1961.
8. Stewart, L. F.: Ballpoint ink age determination by volatile component comparison–a preliminary study. *JFS*, 30: 405, 1985.
9. Lyter, A.H.: Examination of ball pen ink by high-pressure liquid chromatography. *JFS*, 1: 339, 1984.
10. Humecki, H.: Experiments in ballpoint ink aging using infrared spectroscopy. Presented at the International Symposium on Questioned Documents, held at the Forensic Science Research and Training Center, FBI Academy, Quantico, VA., 1985.
11. Hofmann, W.: The dating of documents (with particular references to documents written with ballpoint pens). Unpublished material, 1969.
12. Brunelle, R. L. & Pro, M. J.: A systematic approach to ink identification. *JAOAC*, 55: 823, 1972.
13. Kikuchi, Y.: Examination of the age of the writing of blue-black inks. *Police Science Laboratory Report*, 12: 379, 1959.
14. McNeil, R. J.: Scanning Auger microscopy for dating manuscript inks. Archeological Chem–III, Joseph B. Lambert (Ed.), *Advances in Chemistry Series, No. 205*, ACS, Washington, chapter 13, 255, 1984.
15. Cantu, A. A. & Prough, R. S.: On the relative aging of inks–the solvent extraction technique. *JFS*, 32: 1151, 1987.
16. Cantu, A.A.: Comments on the accelerated aging of inks. *JFS*, 33: 744, 1988.
17. Brunelle, R. L. & Lee, H.: Determining the relative age of ballpoint ink using a single-solvent extraction mass independent approach. *JFS*, 34: 1166, 1989.
18. Brunelle, R. L.: Ink dating: The state of the art. *JFS*, 37: 113, 1992.
19. Brunelle, R. L.: A sequential multiple approach to determining the relative age of writing inks. *Int. J. Forensic Document Examiners*, 1: 94, 1995.
20. Brunelle, R. L. & Speckin, E. J.: Technical report with case studies on the accelerated aging of ballpoint inks. *Int. J. Forensic Document Examiners, 4*: 240, 1998.

Chapter 2

INK ANALYSIS: TRAINING AND INTERDISCIPLINARY COORDINATION

You may use information presented in this book as a guide to tested and peer-reviewed methods of ink analysis. Other standardized procedures are available from the *American Society for Testing and Materials (ASTM) publication E 1422-91, Standard Guide for Forensic Writing Ink Comparison,*[1] and the FBI-supported *Scientific Working Group for Document Examination* (SWGDOC) publication, *Guidelines for the Physical (Non-destructive) Examination of Inks.*[2] Brunelle and Cantu published *Training Requirements and Ethical Responsibilities of Forensic Scientists Performing Ink Dating Examinations in the Journal of Forensic Sciences,* in November, 1987. It may not be necessary to follow each guideline exactly in every case; however, the analyst should be prepared to explain why certain procedures were followed–or omitted.

Refinements in procedures are achieved through peer-reviewed publication of research in forensic science journals and these refinement presentations are frequent topics in workshops and seminars conducted by organizations such as *The American Academy of Forensic Sciences.*

INK ANALYSIS AND FORENSIC DOCUMENT EXAMINATION

Inasmuch as forensic ink analysis usually involves documents, it can be regarded as a specialized area of forensic (or *questioned*) document examination, which itself covers more than a dozen general categories of analyses. On the other hand, some ink analysts are specialists who do not perform other types of document analyses. And then there are instances in which ink analysis is not specifically connected with documents. For instance, we have dealt with cases in which murderers and vandals have written threats or taunts on walls. Matching ink from those writings with known-source markers provided evidence of the writings' source in each case.

In any case, an ink analyst should be familiar with the other fields of forensic science, especially forensic document examination, and how these types of analyses affect the handling of forensic ink evidence. Such awareness will minimize analysis problems arising from the semi-destructive nature of some types of ink analyses, so that a conflict-free sequence of evidence processing can be planned in advance.

Traditionally, the field of forensic document examination involves following types of analyses:

- Identification or elimination of writer by handwriting comparison (not to be confused with "Graphology," which is the purported assessment of personality traits from handwriting)
- Typewriter identification or elimination/product alteration detection
- Photocopier identification or elimination/product alteration detection
- Mechanical printing identification or elimination/product alteration detection
- Paper batch identification
- Charred document restoration
- Latent writing impression restoration
- Physical edge match of documents
- Check protector identification or elimination/product alteration detection
- Rubber stamp identification or elimination/product alteration detection
- Obliteration restoration
- Document preparation sequence determination
- Counterfeit detection
- Image enhancement
- Computer printer identification or elimination/product alteration detection
- Ink analysis

Many of the above analysis techniques will overlap in casework.

COORDINATION WITH HANDWRITING COMPARISONS

Forensic handwriting comparison for identification or elimination of a writer is most revealing when it involves examination of original, unaltered evidence. You should remove ink samples from a document only after required handwriting comparisons have been performed on that document.

One example of a conflict that can occur if this procedure is not followed involves the ink analyst's need to remove ink samples at line intersections, owing to the generally greater quantity of ink present at these sites. Questions may arise concerning the sequence of application of ink lines at such an intersection. Removal of ink from this location may make this determination impossible. Gooping is another site of heavy ink deposition on a ballpoint ink line. It is caused by minute imperfections or debris on the pen tip and it reveals the direction of pen movement. If you remove sites of "gooping" prior to handwriting comparison, you may hinder this aspect of the examination.

Preserving the readability of a questioned document is another consideration. Frequently, analysts working for different parties in civil litigation or defense and prosecution in criminal cases, each remove samples for analysis. If they are not careful, they may remove such a large portion of the written line that not only is handwriting comparison compromised, but entries on a document that are key to the issue under litigation may be rendered unreadable. At best you are then left with only photographic records of key evidence.

If handwriting comparison is, or may be required, consult a competent forensic document examiner prior to ink sampling–if you are not trained in this area. Confer with the case attorney to insure that your plan for ink sampling does not jeopardize the evidentiary value of the document.

COORDINATION WITH LATENT PRINT PROCESSING

If you plan to chemically process a document for latent prints, remove ink samples first to avoid contaminating the ink with latent print developing reagents, e.g., ninhydrin–and to prevent dissolution of the ink on the page by the carrier solvent. One product that may minimize latent print conflicts is a just-released ninhydrin solvent that claims it will not cause ink dissolution. It is called Novec™ Engineered Fluid HFE-7100 from 3M Corporation, distributed by Lightning Powder Co., Inc. of Salem Oregon.

EQUIPMENT ACCESS

There is another aspect of interdisciplinary coordination that may affect a laboratory's budget. In this book, we will discuss a wide variety of ink analysis techniques that together may present a prohibitive investment in instrumentation.

While Forensic Document Sections of crime laboratories seldom have the equipment to perform all of these techniques, many of these instruments are routinely utilized in other sections of a typical full-service crime laboratory. Toxicology and Drug Analysis Sections commonly have mass spectrometers as well as FTIR and Raman spectrometers. DNA sections may perform capillary electrophoresis. Trace evidence sections frequently use visible-range microspectrophotometers. Therefore even though document or ink analysis sections may not be able to justify the cost of expensive equipment, this equipment is usually available in other sections of full-service crime laboratories.

REFERENCES

1. www.astm.org
2. www.for-swg.org/swgdochm.htm

Chapter 3

INK CHEMISTRY

RECOGNIZING INK SOURCE

With experience, the general chemical composition of an ink sample can be predicted by identifying the type of pen (or other device) used to apply the ink. That procedure is covered in Chapter 4, as part of the preliminary analyses of ink.

Examples of Inks and Related Substances
Encountered in Forensic Analysis

- Ballpoint pen ink
- Roller-ball pen ink
- Fiber-tip pen ink
- Marker ink
- Fountain pen ink
- Porous-tip pen ink
- Ink jet printer ink
- Plastic-tip pen ink
- Gel-pen ink
- Pencil
- Rubber stamp ink
- Offset printing ink
- Letterpress ink
- Typewriter ink
- Copier Toner
- Dye-Pack

CHEMICAL COMPOSITION OF INKS

Manufacturers have introduced several types of pens since 1945. Each type offered improvements or differences to address specific market requirements. Forensic ink analysts will encounter ballpoint pen inks more often than any other type of ink. However, the fastest growing group of pens contains gel-ink, which is chemically different from ink of conventional ballpoint pens.

Regardless of the type of pen, writing pen inks contain many different functional categories of ingredients. The majority of these ingredients are organic compounds. Writing ink ingredients include dyes, pigments, solvents, resins, lubricants, biocides, surfactants, corrosion-inhibitors, sequestrants, shear-thinning agents, emulsifying agents, buffers, and many other minor additives to adjust pH, viscosity, polymerization, and also to prevent pen blockage. Gel pens also contain pseudo-plasticizers, which give these inks their unique consistency.

We have presented molecular structure and chemical data[1] for selected ink ingredients; however, you can find such data for most ingredients from these formulations in the many electronic databases available today, including many that are available free-of-charge on the World Wide Web.

Dyes

Dyes are aromatic coloring agents that are normally soluble in organic solvents. Manufacturers use dyes for coloration of a variety of products such as inks, fabric colorants, biological stains, and indicators. You can find technical information on dyes in literature concerning each of these industrial and scientific uses.

The color of dyes is a result of their absorption of a portion of visible electromagnetic radiation. This absorption is caused by energy alteration of delocalized electron systems of the dyes' aromatic structures by atomic configurations called chromophores. Common chromophoric configurations include alternate single and double bonds incorporating nitrogen, carbon, oxygen, or sulphur. Dye color can be enhanced by the addition of ionizing functional groups called auxochromes. Examples include hydroxyl, carboxyl, amino, and sulfonyl.

Dye Classification

The *Colour Index* has been the internationally accepted catalog of dyes and pigments since the *Society of Dyers and Colourists* (SDC) first began publishing the index in 1924. Today, the Colour Index classifies colorants by what it calls "application" or "constitution." There are 19 "applications," which describe such attributes as the type of chromophores (e.g., acid dyes), specific use (e.g., fluorescent brightening agents), or origin (e.g., natural dyes).[2] The 28 constitution designations refer to chemical structure (e.g., triarylmethane).

Different designations may refer to a single colorant. For instance, Solvent Yellow 43 is a Color Index (C.I.) generic name, developed by the *Society of Dyers and Colourists* (SDC) and the *Association of Textile Chemists and Colourists* (AATCC). This same dye may be listed by its *International Union of Pure and Applied Chemistry* (IUPAC) name, 2-butyl-6 (butylamino)-1*H*-benz [*de*] isoquinoline-1, 3(2*H*)-dione. Indexes and catalogs may list dyes by their Chemical Abstracts Services (CAS) number or product name. For this reason, the same dye may be listed under more than one CAS number—one for the C.I. name and one for the IUPAC name.[3]

Although dyes from any SDC dye constitution class could appear in the formulations of writing inks, there are four classes that are of particular interest to ink analysts: arylmethane, azo, phthalocyanine, and azine (nigrosine).

ARYLMETHANE DYES. Arylmethane dyes are derived from methane, with hydrogen atoms replaced by aryl rings. The number of aryl groups is indicated by the prefix in the IUPAC name. Methyl Violet and Methyl Blue are examples of triarylmethane dyes.

AZO DYES. Azo dyes contain the azo chromophore (N=N -). The number of chromophores is indicated by the prefix, where azo is equivalent to monoazo.

Examples of Azo Writing Ink Dyes

Monoazo dyes	*Diazo dyes*
Acid Orange 10	Solvent Black 3
Solvent Black 47	Direct Black 168
Solvent Black 46	Reactive Black 31
Solvent Yellow 162	Amido Black 10B
Solvent Yellow 82	Reactive Yellow 37
Reactive Black 31	Reactive Red 180

PHTHALOCYANINE DYES. Phthalocyanine dyes have a complex structure based upon a tetrabenzoporphyrazine nucleus. These dyes form metal complexes, the most stable of which are formed with transition metals, especially copper. These are large molecules, the properties of which are adjusted by sulfonation. Most phthalocyanine dyes are either 2 or 3 sulfonated, with mixtures of the two designated to reflect the ratio, e.g., 2.4 sulfonated phthalocyanine.[4]

Examples of Phthalocyanine Writing Ink Dyes

Copper Phthalocyanine   Solvent Blue 38
Solvent Blue 64   Solvent Blue 70

Most blue ballpoint ink formulations made since the 1960s contain metalized dyes such as copper phthalocyanine. These dyes are both colorfast and highly soluble in glycols, the most common group of ballpoint pen ink solvents. The manufacturer may adjust the color of this blue dye with "shading dyes."

NIGROSINE WRITING INK DYES. Nigrosine dyes are acid dyes, described in the literature as being of the azine (pyridine) or aniline (aminobenzene) chemical classes. Nigrosines are blue to black in color. Black glycol inks contain soluble dye combinations that appear black in the written line or they contain soluble nigrosines.[5] Nigrosines are also reported to be "dirty" dyes as they are used in inks, with many contaminants, especially metals.

Dye Solubility

You can find information on solubility of many writing ink dyes in *Physico-Chemical Principles of Color Chemistry* (A.T. Peters & H. S. Freeman, 1996; ISBN 0 7514-0210-9).

Dye Fading

Chapters 8 and 9 describe how measurements of dye fading can be used to date inks. Also, methods of accelerated aging of inks by UV irradiation are under current study and are covered in Chapter 9.

The mechanisms of dye fading are not completely understood because of the many factors involved. Most of the published studies to date have been provided by researchers in the textile industry. While some of their data is pertinent to writing inks, other textile industry data comes from dye degradation on textile fibers, not paper. This must be kept in mind because chemical composition of the substrate can affect dye degradation.

Dyes can undergo photosensitized oxidation and this photo-fading is influenced by moisture, atmosphere, temperature, and aggregation, as well as by the chemical structure both of the dye and the substrate.[6] Moisture, in general, increases the rate of dye degradation.[7] The wavelength and power of the light with which the dyes are irradiated also affect the rate of fading. Azo dyes have also been shown to undergo reductive photodegradation[8] and photo as well as thermal trans-cis isomerization.[9]

Triphenylmethane dyes exhibit relatively low lightfastness. Crystal Violet and Malachite Green, exposed to a mercury vapor lamp for a few days have been shown to undergo color changes and eventually yield colorless products. The rate of degradation of these dyes is accelerated by the presence of a singlet oxygen sensitizer, e.g., Methylene Blue.[10]

Andrasko reported in 2001 that Crystal Violet and Methyl Violet in ballpoint inks on paper decompose when exposed to sunlight. The decomposition apparently involves successive loss of methyl groups, yielding decomposition products that were detected using HPLC with detection at 540 nm.[11]

Phthalocyanines are said to be the most stable of all colorants in use today.[12]

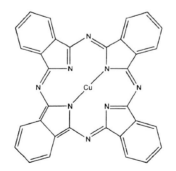

Figure 3.1. Copper phthalocyanine ink dye.

Copper Phthalocyanine Chemical Data

- Empirical formula: $C_{32}H_{16}CuN_8$
- Molecular weight: 576.078

- Synonyms: Accosperse cyan blue GT; Aqualine blue; Arloc-
  yanine blue PS; Bahama blue BC; Congo blue B 4; Copper (II)
  phthalocyanine; Copper beta-phthalocyanine; alpha-Copper
  phthalocyanine; eta-Copper phthalocyanine; Copper phthalocyanine blue; Copper tetrabenzoporphyrazine

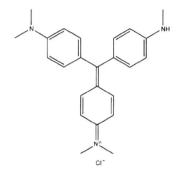

Figure 3.2. Methyl violet–pentamethyl pararosanilin homologue (ink dye).

Methyl Violet is formed from mixtures of tetramethyl pararosanilin,
pentamethyl pararosanilin, and hexamethyl pararosanilin (Crystal
Violet). Manufacturers may use methyl violet comprised of different
homologue ratios and regard the variations as a component of one ink
formulation.

Methyl Violet Chemical Data

- Empirical formulas of homologues: $C_{23}H_{26}N_3Cl$; $C_{24}H_{28}N_3Cl$;
  $C_{25}H_{30}N_3Cl$, respectively
- Molecular weights of homologues: 379.942; 393.969; 407.996,
  respectively
- Synonyms: Methyl Violet 2B, Gentian Violet (may refer to many
  dyes of the class)

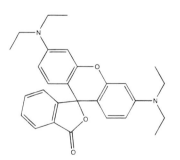

Figure 3.3. Solvent red 49 (ink dye).

Solvent Red Chemical Data

- Empirical formula: $C_{28}H_{30}N_3$
- Molecular weight: 442.5566
- Synonyms: Rhodamine B base; spiro[isobenzofuran-1(3H),9'-[9H] xanthen]-3-one, 3',6'-bis(diethylamino)

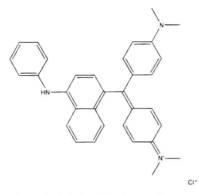

Figure 3.4. Victoria blue (ink dye).

Victoria Blue Chemical Data

- Empirical Formula: $C_{33}H_{32}ClN_3$
- Molecular weight: 506.0889
- Synonyms: Victoria Blue B; N-[4-[[4-(dimethylamino)phenyl][4-(phenylamino)-1-naphthyl]methylene]-2,5-cyclohexadien-1-ylidene]-N-methyl-chloride

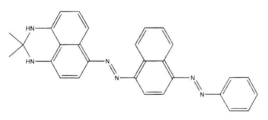

Figure 3.5. Solvent black 3 (ink dye).

Solvent Black 3 Chemical Data

- Empirical formula: $C_{29}H_{24}N_6$
- Molecular weight: 456.559
- Synonym: Sudan Black B

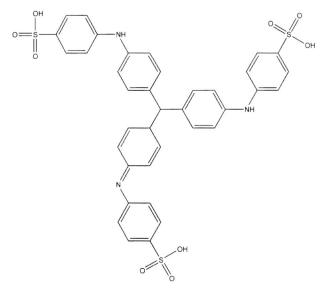

Figure 3.6. Methyl blue (ink dye).

Methyl Blue Chemical Data

- Empirical formula: $C_{37}H_{27}N_3O_9S_3Na_2$
- Molecular weight: 799.81
- Synonyms: Cotton blue, Helvetia blue

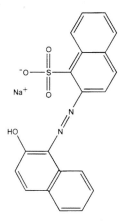

Figure 3.7. Lithol red (ink dye).

Lithol Red Chemical Data

- Empirical formula: $C_{20}H_{13}N_2NaO_4S$
- Formula weight: 400.38347

- Synonyms: D & C red no. 10; 1-Naphthalenesulfonic acid, 2-[(2-hydroxy-1-naphthyl)azo]-monosodium salt

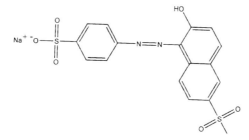

Figure 3.8. Food yellow (ink dye).

Food Yellow 3 Chemical Data

- Empirical formula: $C_{16}H_{10}N_2Na_2O_7S_2$
- Molecular weight: 452.36374
- Synonym: Disodium salt of 1-p-sulfophenylazo-2-naphthol-6-sulfonic acid

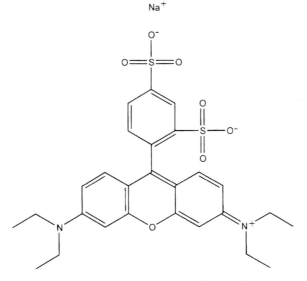

Figure 3.9. Acid red 52 (ink dye).

Acid Red 52 Chemical Data

- Empirical formula: $C_{27}H_{29}N_2NaO_7S_2$
- Molecular weight: 580.64507

- Synonyms: Food Red No.106; Sulfo Rhodamine B; Xanthylium; Sodium 9-(2,4-disulfonatophenyl)-3,6-bis(diethylamino) xanthylium

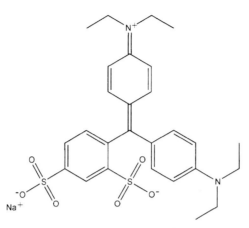

Figure 3.10. Acid blue 1 (ink dye).

Acid Blue 1 Chemical Data

- Empirical formula: $C_{27}H_{31}N_2NaO_6S_2$
- Molecular weight: 566.66147
- Synonyms: Patent Blue VF; Ethanaminium N-[4-[[4-(diethylamino)phenyl](2,4-disulfophenyl)methylene]-2,5-cyclohexadien-1-ylidene]-N-ethyl-inner salt, sodium salt

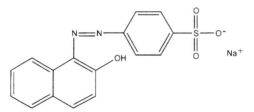

Figure 3.11. Acid orange 10 (ink dye).

Acid Orange 10 Chemical Data

- Empirical formula: $C_{16}H_{10}N_2O_7S_2Na_2$
- Molecular weight: 452.386

Ink jet printer inks, which are similar to roller-ball inks, contain dyes and dye complexing agents. A common ink jet dye complexing agent is vinyl pyrrolidinone (Fig. 3.12).

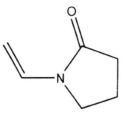

Figure 3.12. Vinyl pyrrolidinone (ink jet dye complexing agent).

Vinyl pyrrolidinone Chemical Data

- Empirical formula: C_6H_9NO
- Molecular weight: 111.1432
- Synonyms: 1-vinyl-2-pyrrolidinone; vinylbutyrolactam

Pigments

Pigments include natural or synthetic, organic or inorganic coloring agents. Unlike dyes, pigments are manufactured as relatively insoluble finely divided particulate powders suspended in a liquid vehicle. Some compounds can be either pigments or dyes, depending upon their form. An example is copper phthalocyanine, which is a dye in its free form and a pigment, Blue 15, as a "precipitated dyestuff pigment."

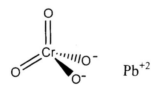

Figure 3.13. Pigment green 15 (ink pigment).

Pigment Green 15 Chemical Data

- Empirical formula: CrO_4Pb
- Molecular weight: 323.1936
- Synonyms: Lead (II) Chromate; Lead (IV) Chromate; Chrome Yellow; Plumbous Chromate

Pigments are classified by generic name (e.g., Pigment Blue 15) or constitution number (e.g., 77007). Pigments are designated by C.I. constitution numbers 11640-77999.[13]

Solvents and Vehicles

The solvents contained in ink formulations may be primarily water, or entirely organic solvents. Water is not generally used as a solvent in glycol-based inks, but can be contained in these inks (as a quality control limit) of up to about 10 percent by weight. Glycol solvents are the most commonly used in what are termed "ballpoint" pens, although benzyl alcohol has also become a common solvent used in ballpoints manufactured by Bic and in other brands marketed throughout Europe. The principle change in ballpoint ink solvents in the last 15 years has been the elimination of toluene.[14] Some of the common writing pen solvents and vehicles are illustrated below.

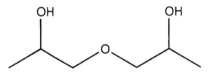

Figure 3.14. Dipropylene glycol.

Dipropylene glycol Chemical Data

- Empirical formula: $C_6H_{14}O_3$
- Molecular weight: 134.1748
- Synonym: Oxybispropanol

Figure 3.15. Butylene glycol.

Butylene glycol Chemical Data

- Empirical formula: $C_4H_{10}O_2$
- Molecular weight: 90.1218
- Synonyms: 1,4-butanediol; 1,4-butylene glycol; 1,4-dihydroxybutane; 1,4-tetramethylene; tetramethylene glycol; butanediol; butane-1,4-diol; 1,4-tetramethylene glycol; tetramethylene-1,4-diol

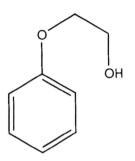

Figure 3.16. Phenyl glycol.

Phenyl glycol Chemical Data

- Empirical formula: $C_8H_{10}O_2$
- Molecular weight: 138.1658
- Synonyms: 2-phenoxyethanol; phenoxetol; phenoxyethyl alcohol; ethylene glycol phenyl ether; hydroxy-2-phenoxyethane; b-hydroxyethyl phenyl ether; ethylene glycol mono phenyl ether

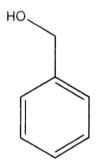

Figure 3.17. Benzyl alcohol.

Benzyl alcohol Chemical Data

- Empirical formula: $C_6H_5CH_2OH$
- Molecular weight: 108.14
- Synonyms: Benzenemethanol, benzenecarbinol; alpha-hydroxy-toluene; phenylmethyl alcohol; phenyl carbinol

Dioctyl phthalate (Fig. 3.18) is a non-volatile erasable ballpoint ink solvent.

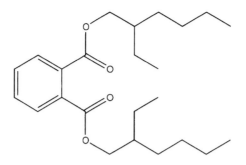

Figure 3.18. Dioctyl phthalate (DEPH).

Dioctyl phthalate Chemical Data

- Empirical formula: $C_{24}H_{38}O_4$
- Molecular weight: 390.5618
- Synonyms: DEHP; DOP; di-sec-octyl phthalate; 2-benzenedicarboxylic acid bis(2-ethylhexyl) ester; Ethyl hexyl phthalate; 2-Ethylhexyl phthalate

Examples of gel-pen vehicles are N-methyl-2-pyrrolidone (Fig. 3.19) and 1,3-dimethyl-2-imidazolidinone (Fig. 3.20).

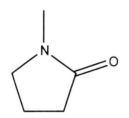

Figure 3.19. N-Methyl-2-pyrrolidone.

N-Methyl-2-pyrrolidone Chemical Data

- Empirical formula: C_5H_9NO
- Molecular weight: 99.1322
- Synonyms: 1-methyl-2-pyrrolidinone; methylpyrrolidone; 1-methyl-5-pyrrolidinone; N-methylpyrrolidone; 1-methyl-2-pyrrolidone

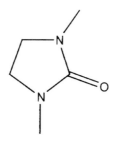

Figure 3.20. 1,3-Dimethyl-2-imidazolidinone.

1,3-Dimethyl-2-imidazolidinone Chemical Data

- Empirical formula: $C_5H_{10}N_2O$
- Molecular weight: 114.1468
- Synonyms: N,N'-dimethylethyleneurea; DMI; DMEU

Resins

Resins are fusible substances of relatively high molecular weight. They can be solid or amorphous semi-solids. They are soluble in organic solvents but not in water. Resins may be derived from either tree secretions or they may be synthesized by polymerization of any of a number of monomers. Ink manufacturers use resins for adjusting the viscosity of ballpoint ink and for increasing film strength and lubricant qualities of the ink as it flows onto the ball. Additionally, as they dry, resins create a chemical bond between the ink and the paper. Some resins (as in the gel ink formulation No. 2 below) impart color to the ink. Resins may be used alone or in a mixture of resins in an ink formulation. Many examples of resins, including the functional groups of their monomers, are given below under the section on ink formulations. Resins are not detected by thin layer chromatography but may be detected by Fourier transform infrared spectroscopy. The latter spectra can show absorption peaks characteristic of the resin's functional groups (see Chapter 6).

Examples of the resin content of some ballpoint pen ink formulations from 1978 to 1999 are shown below. Each formulation calls for a combination from the choices of resins listed.

Resin Classes and Year of Introduction

1978

Coal tar, coumarone, coumarone-indene, phenol-modified-coumarone, phenol-modified-coumarone-indene, hexanetriol phthalate resin, ketone condensate, ketone-aldehyde condensate, pine tar, polyvinylpyrrolidone, and zein.[15]

1994

Ketone resins; Aldehyde resins, e.g., acetophenone/formaldehyde resins; Phenolic resins, e.g., completely condensed phenolic formaldehyde resins.[16]
Oil-free alkyd and polyester resins.

1999

Ketone, sulfonamide, maleic, xylene, alkyd resins.
Phenolic and rosin resins.
Ester gums.[17]

Monomers of one ballpoint ink copolymer resin (Commercial name: RJ-101) are illustrated in Figure 3.21.

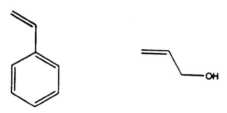

Figure 3.21. Styrene and allyl alcohol.

Styrene Chemical Data

• Empirical formula: C_8H_8
• Molecular weight: 104.1512

Allyl Alcohol Chemical Data

• Empirical formula: C_3H_6O
• Molecular weight: 58.0798

Lubricants

Lubricants are added to permit the ball in the point socket to rotate freely. A common lubricant found in ballpoint pen inks patented in the last 20 years is oleic acid, which is also used as a drying agent and to adjust the viscosity of the ink.

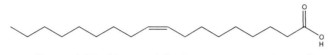

Figure 3.22. Oleic acid (ballpoint pen ink lubricant).

Oleic acid Chemical Data

- Empirical formula: $C_{18}H_{34}O_2$
- Molecular weight: 282.4654
- Synonyms: Cis-delta-9-octadecanoate; 9-octadecenoic acid (Z); cis-9-octadecenoic acid; cis-octadec-9-enoic acid

Other Ink Ingredients

Biocides are added to some formulations to prevent microbial growth in the ink. Surfactants adjust surface tension of the mixture and insure that the ink is capable of wetting the metal used in the tip of the pen to produce an acceptable delivery rate of ink to the writing surface.

Corrosion-inhibitors preserve the metal ball and point socket. Sequestrants are substances that hold a substance (e.g., a metallic ion) in solution by complexing action. In ink formulations, they are used for stabilizing some of the water-dispersible polymeric thickeners.[18] Shear thinning agents permit flow through the ball of a ballpoint or fiber tip of the marker pen. Tertiary-butyl hydroperoxide (Fig. 3.23) is a preservative and diluting agent used in water-based ink for rollerball pens. It is commonly used as a 70% solution in water.

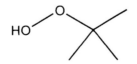

Figure 3.23. Tertiary-butyl hydroperoxide.

Tertiary-butyl Hydroperoxide Chemical Data

- Empirical formula: $C_4H_{10}O_2$
- Molecular weight: 90.1218
- Synonyms: TBHP; 2-hydroperoxy-2-methylpropane; dimethy-lethyl hydroperoxide; Slimicide DE-488.

Emulsifying agents, diluting agents, preservatives, buffers, and additives to adjust pH, viscosity, polymerization, and prevent pen blockage–do what their names suggest.

A ballpoint ink formulation introduced in 1999 included the addition of 7 to 40 nm diameter silica particles dispersed by polyvinylpyrrolidone to prevent ink from leaking out of the pen tip. This process created a smooth writing feeling and elimination of clogging at the pen tip.[19]

INK FORMULATIONS

The following are a number of ink formulations commonly used in pens today, along with some related products. These formulations include many ingredient options. Not all of the substances listed under each category are necessarily found in one ink. Selections of these ingredients or combinations thereof can make up some ink formulations on the market today.

We have provided these formulations to facilitate the interpretation of data from analysis of inks written on documents and to indicate which new techniques may be useful for ink analysis.

As these lists demonstrate, inks are not pure substances. Therefore spectra obtained by FTIR of inks represent superimposed spectra of many different organic compounds–which can present a problem resolving peaks. Thin layer chromatography primarily reveals separated dye components but does not detect other substances.

Ingredients below are listed by the product names, common names or chemical names. Other ingredients are listed by generic, product, or chemical name and may be found in available electronic databases. Note: U.S. Patents cover all of the following ink formulations.

Ballpoint Pen Inks

Ballpoint Ink Example 1

This ballpoint ink formulation,[20] introduced August, 1999, uses benzyl alcohol as the primary solvent and variations on the formulation may include either dyes or pigments or a combination.

DYES. Balifast Color (brand name, manufactured by Orient Chemical Ind. Co., Ltd.), and Aizen Spiron dye and Aizen SOT dye (brand names, manufactured by Hodogaya Chemical Ind. Co., Ltd.). Dyes comprise 5.0–20.0 % of the ink by weight.

PIGMENTS. Inorganic pigments such as titanium oxide, carbon black and metal powder, and organic pigments such as azo lakes, insoluble azo pigments, chelate azo pigments, phthalocyanine pigments, perylene pigments, anthraquinone pigments, quinacridone pigments, dye lakes, nitro pigments, and nitroso pigments.

ORGANIC SOLVENTS. Benzyl alcohol, phenoxyethanol, carbitols and cellosolves. (They may be used alone or in a mixture.)

RESINS. Ketone resins, sulfonamide resins, maleic resins, ester gums, xylene resins, alkyd resins, phenol resins and rosin resins. (ca. 8.0 % of the ink by weight).

LUBRICANTS. Oleic acid (5.0% by weight).

ADDITIVE (Anti-clogging/blobbing) Polyvinylpyrrolidone (4.0% by weight), Lubiscol K-90 manufactured by BASF CO., Ltd.

Ballpoint Pen Ink Example 2

Introduced May, 1994,[21] its innovation was it exhibited superior writing characteristics and did not leak, even at very low and very high ambient temperatures and very high humidity.

DYES. (15 to 35% by weight) Cationic dyes, such as Astra, Brilliant and Victoria blue bases Soluble phthalocyanine bases (for blue ink). Copper phthalocyanine base with a nigrosine base (for black ink).

LUBRICANT. Oleic acid (Also solubilizes cationic dyes).

RESINS AND BINDERS.
• Option 1: Ketone resins and aldehyde resins, such as acetophenone/formaldehyde resins, hydrogenated acetophenone/formaldehyde resins, urethanized cetophenone/formaldehyde resins, ethylene urea/formaldehyde resins, isobutyralde-

hyde/ urea/formaldehyde resins, cyclohexanone/formaldehyde resins, alkyl cyclohexanone/formaldehyde resins, cyclohexanone resins, and methyl ethyl ketone/formaldehyde resins.
- Option 2: Phenolic resins, e.g., completely condensed phenolic formaldehyde resins, termed "novolaks."
- Option 3: Oil-free alkyd and polyester resins.

Additionally, these different resins can also be used in combination.

SOLVENTS. Glycols, glycol ethers, aliphatic glycol ethers, and alcohols. Examples are phenyl glycol, 1,2-propane diol, ethylene diglycol, butylene diglycol, dipropylene glycol, 2-ethyl-1, 3-hexane diol, diethylene glycol, triethylene glycol, phenoxyethanol, and benzyl alcohol. Fatty acids, such as oleic acid.

THICKENERS. Polyvinyl pyrrolidone or mineral oil thickened with aluminum stearate.

ADDITIVES. 0.01 to 10% by weight of an alcohol-soluble cellulose derivative, e.g., alcohol-soluble cellulose esters and cellulose ethers (to adjust viscosity and temperature behavior).

Ballpoint Pen Ink No. 3

Manufactured by Mitsubishi Pencil Kabushiki Kaisha,[22] Tokyo, and introduced in December, 1999, this non-aqueous ink for ballpoint pens is designed to provide superior "cap-off" performance. This means that writing performance does not deteriorate even when the pen is allowed to stand with the cap off. It is also designed to eliminate "blobbing" or "gooping." The latter accomplished by addition of an autolyophobic vehicle (an organic solvent having a vapor pressure of 0.2 mm Hg at 20° C or less), which can inhibit a tip holder from wetting. The formation of ink drops, which causes blobbing, is suppressed. Solvents with autolyophobic properties include 1-octanol, 2-octanol, benzyl alcohol, ethylene glycol monophenyl ether, diethylene glycol, monomethyl ether, and 2-ethyl-1-hexanol. An additive is added to the solvent to further increase the autolyophobic properties.

ORGANIC SOLVENTS. Dipropylene glycol, benzyl alcohol, propylene glycol monophenyl ether, triethylene glycol monobutyl ether, tripropylene glycol monomethyl ether, octyl adipate, dibutyl sebacate, dioctyl sebacate, glycerin, polypropylene glycol polyoxypropyltriol, ethylene glycol monophenyl ether, ethylene glycol monobenzyl ether, 1-octanol, 2-octanol, 2-ethyl-1-hexanol, et al. Total organic solvent =

50 to 95% by weight based on the weight of the ink.

OLEOPHOBIC ADDITIVES. Perfluoroalkylphosphoric acid esters and alkylphosphoric acid esters.

COLORANTS. Dyes including Barifast Black #1802, Barifast Black #1805, Barifast Black #3820, Barifast Violet #1701, Barifast Yellow AUM and Barifast Yellow #3104 (Orient Chemical Industry Co., Ltd.), Spiron Violet C-RH, Spiron Black CMH Special, Spiron Yellow C-GNH, Spiron Orange GRH, and Spiron Red BEH. (Hodogaya Chemical Co., Ltd.), Auramines, Rhodamines, Methyl Violets, Malachite Greens, Crystal Violets and Victoria Blues.

PIGMENTS. Titanium oxide, carbon black, phthalocyanine compounds, azo compounds, anthraquinone compounds, quinacridone compounds, Microlease Color (made by Ciba-Geigy) and Fuji AS Color (made by Fuji Dyestuff Co., Ltd.).

PIGMENT DISPERSANT. Polyvinyl butyrals, polyvinyl pyrrolidones, polyacrylic acids, styrene-maleic acid resins. Solsperses made by ICI, which are the resins and oligomers, and Eslec B BM-1 and Eslec B BL-1 (Sekisui Chemical Co., Ltd.) which are the polyvinyl butyrals. An anionic, a nonionic or a cationic surface active agent, may be added as a main component or an auxiliary component. Amount: 0.1 to 40% by weight based on the weight of the pigment and in the 0.05 to 20% by weight based on the total weight of the ink.

COAGULANT. Synthesized fine powder silica, bentonites, extremely fine precipitated calcium carbonate. Amount: 0.01 to 10%, preferably 0.5 to 5%.

Gel-Pen Inks

Gel-pens have rapidly become a prominent type of pen due to their smooth writing characteristics, and because they are inexpensive to manufacture. Also, these inks are practically indestructible on paper. Manufacturers expect gel inks to continue to hold a considerable proportion of the writing pen market. Therefore, forensic ink analysts will see gel inks with increasing frequency. This brings up a problem for ink analysts–gel inks are often difficult or impossible to analyze using thin layer chromatography due to the fact that the colorants of gel pen ink are often limited to pigments–rather than the soluble dye components that yield such excellent chromatograms from conventional ballpoint pens.

Gel Pen Ink Example Number 1

Introduced in 1999, this gel-pen ink[23] was developed by a Japanese manufacturer to provide a pen with the characteristics of a free-flowing ink. Its roller ball produces little blobbing and is capable of drawing stable lines with vivid color and no uneven intensity of written lines. The gel-pen accomplishes this through a pseudoplasticity of the ink, i.e., the characteristic that the viscosity of a relatively low viscosity aqueous ink is lowered by the rotation of the ball point to allow the ink to flow out smoothly. Pseudoplasticity is associated with a "shear-thinning viscosity."

VEHICLES. Water and a water-soluble organic solvent or solvents, e.g., alkylene glycols, polyalkylene glycols, triols, glycerols, thiodiethanol, N-methyl-2-pyrrolidone and 1,3-dimethyl-2-imidazolidinone. Pseudoplasticizer xanthan gum, tamarind gum, carrageenan gum, tragacanth gum, locust bean gum, gum arabic, guar gum, curdlan, pectin, agar, gelatin, mannans, and cellulose, and from acrylic synthetic polymers, urethane synthetic polymers, smectite, and montmorillonite, methyl cellulose, ethyl cellulose, and carboxymethyl cellulose.

RESINS. Carboxymethyl cellulose and xanthan gum.

INORGANIC PIGMENTS. Titanium oxide, carbon black and metal powder, and organic pigments including, azo lakes, insoluble azo pigments, chelate azo pigments, phthalocyanine pigments, perylene and perinone pigments, anthraquinone pigments, quinacridone pigments, dye lakes, and nitroso pigments.

NONIONIC SURFACTANTS. Polyoxyalkylene higher fatty acid esters, higher fatty acid partial esters of polyhydric alcohols, and higher fatty acid esters of saccharide. Anionic surfactants Alkylated sulfonates of higher fatty acid amides and alkylallylsulfonates.

FOOD DYES. E.g., C.I. Food Yellow 3.

BASIC DYES. C.I. Basic Yellow 1, C.I. Basic Orange 2, C.I. Basic Violet 1 C.I. Basic green 4.

ADDITIONAL INGREDIENTS. Lubricants, rust preventives, antiseptics, and pH controllers may be found in this ink.

Gel Ink Example Number 2

Introduced January 27, 1998 by Sakura Color Products Corporation,[24] Osaka, Japan, it is termed an "aqueous ballpoint ink."

It employs coloring materials consisting of a pigment with a pigment dispersant, with an optional colored emulsion resin. It uses a water-soluble organic solvent, a "pseudoplastic imparting agent," water, and a cross-linked polyacrylate salt.

COLORANTS. Azo pigment, condensed polyazo pigment, phthalocyanine pigment, quinacridone pigment, anthraquinone pigment, dioxazine pigment, indigoid pigment, thioindigoid pigment, perinone, perylene pigment, organic pigments, e.g., melamine pigment and titanium oxide, iron oxide, carbon black optional colored emulsion resins, e.g., LUMICOL #2100' series "LUMICOL #3000' series (trademark, product of NIPPON KEIKO KAGAKU Co., LTD.).

RESINS. Water-soluble acrylic resin, synthetic resins, water-soluble maleic acid resin, water-soluble styrene resin, water-soluble styrene-acrylic resin, water-soluble styrene-maleic acid resin, polyvinyl pyrrolidone, polyvinyl alcohol, and water-soluble urethane resin.

ORGANIC SOLVENTS. Two or more of the following (1%–40% by weight) ethylene glycol, diethylene glycol, propylene glycol, glycerin, and like polyhydric alcohols; propylene glycol monomethyl ether and like glycolethers; propylene glycol monomethyl ether acetate and like glycol ether esters.

PSEUDOPLASTIC IMPRATING AGENTS. Natural polysaccharides, e.g., Welan gum and/or xanthan gum, cyamoposis gum, locust bean gum, and ramsan gum having polymeric formula composed of monosaccharides such as glucose, galactose, rhamnose, mannose, glucuronate salt, and semi-synthetic cellulose polymers.

SEMI-SYNTHETIC CELLUOSE POLYMERS. An example is a polyacrylate polymer, identified by trademarks, e.g., "THEOGIC 250H (NIHON JUNYAKU CO., LTD), "JUNLON PW111" (NIHON JUNYAKU CO., LTD), "U-Jelly CP" (SHOWA DENKO K.K.), "CARBOPOL #934" (B.F. Goodrich Company).

pH ADJUSTING AGENTS. Sodium hydroxide, sodium carbonate, alkanol amine, and ammonia.

LUBRICANTS. Alkali metal salts or alkanol amine salts of fatty acids and phosphorous surfactants.

RUST PREVENTIVES. Benzotriazole, derivatives thereof, and dicyclohexylammonium nitrate.

ANTISEPTICS. Potassium sorbate, sodium benzoate, sodium pentachlorophenolate, sodium dihydroacetate, 1,2-benzisothiazoline-3-on.

Specific Example of a Preparation Using the Above Generalized Formulation

Component	Percentage
Copper(II) phthalocyanine blue	4.0
Styrene-acrylate copolymer sodium salt (pigment dispersant)	1.0
Diethylene glycol	10.0
Glycerin	5.0
Crosslinked-type acrylate copolymer sodium salt	0.1 (not counted in %)
1,2-Benzisothiazoline-3-on	0.5
Benzotriazole	0.5
Xanthan gum	0.3
Water	78.7

Gel-Pen Ink Example 3

Introduced in 1995 by National Ink Incorporated, this is a fluid ink[25] but contains a substantially reduced amount of water compared to earlier formulations–4% by weight of water if the ink utilizes dye as the colorant and as little as 10% by weight of water–if the ink utilizes pigment as the colorant. It features a polymeric material (e.g., a chemically modified hydrocarbon) to produce superior "cap off" properties. It features shear-thinning fluids containing high levels of polar non-aqueous, high-boiling-point liquids.

VEHICLES. Aqueous solution containing ethylene glycol.

SHEAR-THINNING AGENTS. Polymeric material, e.g., alpha-methyl-styrene-styrene-acrylic acid terpolymer.

COLORANTS. Direct Violet 99, Basonyl RTM. Blue 636, Direct Blue 86, Regal 330R Carbon Black, Fast Light Orange 2GM, titanium dioxide, Carmine 6B, Pigment Red 112, Pigment Blue 15, Pigment Green 7, Direct Blue 71, Direct Black 19, Acid Red 92.

POLYMERIC THICKENERS. Xanthan, carboxymethylcellulose.

SEQUESTRANTS. Tetrasodium EDTA or Versene 100 RTM of Dow Chemical, trisodium phosphate, sodium hexametaphosphate, or sodium glucoheptanate.

BIOCIDES. Methyl *p*-hydroxybenzoate, propyl *p*-hydroxybenzoate, 1-(3-hloroallyl)-3,5,7-triazo-1-azoniaadamantane chloride.

CORROSION INHIBITORS. Benzotriazole, tolyltriazole, dicyclohexyl ammonium nitrate.

WETTING AGENTS. Surfactants, e.g., sodium lauryl sulfate, fluorinated alkyl esters.

pH CONTROLLERS. Triethanolamine, morpholine, diethanolamine, ethylamine, or monoethylamine.

Ink for Roller-Ball Pens

Introduced in 1998, this ink[26] may be found in fountain pens, roller ball pens, felt-tip pens, or ink jet printer cartridges.

SOLVENT. Ethylene glycol.

BINDING AGENTS. Hydrocolloid/hydrocolloids or polysaccharide/polysaccharides (Hydrocolloids form hydrogels with water which dry up to form protective films).

MOIST-KEEPING AGENTS. Diethylene glycol, glycerine, propylene glycol, or polyglycol.

BUFFER. Triethanol amine.

PRESERVATIVE. Tertiary butyl hydroperoxide and monophenyl glycol ether.

EMULSIFYING AGENTS. Bees wax, alcohol fatty acid ester, ethylene fatty acid ester, polyethylene glycol fatty acid ester.

PEN BLOCK PREVENTATIVES. Inorganic salts, organic salts or other organic compounds, amino acids, urea, sulfur compounds.

FOOD DYES. Food Yellow 3; Food Yellow 13; Food Yellow 4; Food Red 7; Food Red 14; E 133, Blue 2 and/or Food Blue 3 and/or 2. Acid dyes form the group: Acid Yellow 23; Acid Red 18; Red 51; Acid Orange 4; Acid Blue 93; Acid Blue 9; Acid Blue 104 and/or Acid Violet 49.

DILUTING AGENTS. Tertiary butyl hydroperoxide, monophenyl glycol ether. The formulation uses no tensides (cross-linking agents).

Ink for Ink Jet Printer

Introduced in 2000, this ink jet printer ink[27] from Xerox features improved shelf stability. Like other ink jet inks, it can be analyzed by thin layer chromatography and chromatograms often resemble those of ballpoint pen inks.[28] The similarity in composition can be seen by comparing the formulations of each listed here. Note, however, that other ink jet formulations may include pigments, precluding extraction, and TLC analysis.[29] Dyes such as Food Black 2 are water-soluble, a requirement for ink jet printers, since water is commonly the primary solvent and ink components must remain in solution to keep from plugging the jet mechanism.[30]

VEHICLE. Water and/or ethylene glycol, diethylene glycols, propylene glycol, glycerine, dipropylene glycols, polyethylene glycols, polypropylene glycols, ethers, amides, urea, substituted ureas, ethers, carboxylic acids and their salts, esters, alcohols, organosulfides, organosulfoxides, sulfones, alcohol derivatives, carbitol, butyl carbitol, cellusolve, tripropylene glycol monomethyl ether, ether derivatives, amino alcohols, ketones, N-methylpyrrolidinone, 2-pyrrolidinone, cyclohexylpyrrolidone, hydroxyethers, amides, sulfoxides, lactones, polyelectrolytes, methyl sulfonylethanol, imidazole, betaine, et al.

ANIONIC DYES. Food Black No. 1, Food Black No. 2, Food Red No. 40, Food Blue No. 1, Food Yellow No. 7, FD & C dyes, Acid Black dyes, et al.

DYE-COMPLEXING AGENT. Any polyquaternized polyvinylamines, polyquaternized polyallylamines, epichlorohydrin/amine copolymers, cationic amido amine copolymers, copolymers of vinyl pyrrolidinone, and a vinyl imidazolium salt. (One theory holds that the polyquaternary amine and the dye form a multidentate ionic complex when mixed the other ink ingredients.)

SURFACTANTS. Alkyl (linear) diphenyl oxide disulfonates, e.g., CAL-FAX 10L-45, from Pilot, Santa Fe Springs, California.

Some variations of this formulation may include various salts to stabilize the vehicle or to participate in ionic cross-linking, thereby enhancing waterfastness of the ink.

Erasable Ballpoint Ink

Scripto, Inc. and Papermate introduced this erasable ballpoint ink formulation[31] around 1982. Its innovation was its initial erasability by ordinary pencil erasers–after which it became a permanent ink. It accomplishes this through the use of both volatile solvents, with a boiling point less than 180° C, and non-volatile, low-viscosity solvents.

ELASTOMERIC POLYMER. Cis-1,4-Polyisoprene (24% by weight).

VOLATILE SOLVENT. Lacquer Diluent #6 (28.5% by weight).

NON-VOLATILE SOLVENT. Dioctyl Phthalate (3.5% by weight).

PIGMENTS. Victoria Blue, Alkali Blue, Phthalo Blue, Lithol Red, Red 2B, graphite, carbon black, and Diarylide Yellow (18% by weight).

LUBRICANTS. Mixture of Oleic, Lauric, and Stearic Acids (1,2,2% by weight, respectively).

Fountain Pen Ink

Fountain pen inks are not as abundant as ballpoint pen inks and other non-ballpoint pen inks but they are often used to sign important documents, and may require forensic analysis.

Typical Fountain Pen Ink Formulation[32]

Water	91%–96%
Synthetic Dyes	1%–5%
Humectant	Less than 2%
Iron Compounds	0%–1%
Tannic Acid	0%–0.5%
Phenol Compounds	Less than 0.5%

Disappearing Ink

Disappearing ink, a common "gag" product, has been known to be used in crimes, such as the scam of writing a check, only to have the ink disappear later. This type of ink commonly consists of a solution of thymophthalein, which is blue in solutions that are basic. When exposed to air, the solvent evaporates, leaving the thymolphthalein (Fig. 3.24) in a neutral state, causing it to become colorless, and appearing to disappear. Throckmorton reported in 1990 that disappearing ink became visible when treated with any alkaline solution.[33]

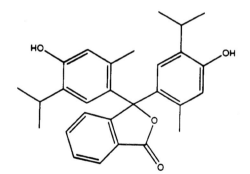

Figure 3.24. Thymolphthalein.

Thymolphthalein Chemical Data

- Empirical formula: $C_{18}H_{30}O_4$
- Molecular weight: 430.54

Dye Pack

A red stain used to mark stolen currency, dye pack contains 1-methylaminoanthraquinone (MAAQ) as well as potentially other dyes.[34] Analysis of Dye Pack is discussed in Chapter 6.

Pencil

As an ink analyst, you will likely be asked to compare questioned pencil entries on a document at some point in your career. The "lead" of pencil is composed of graphite, clays, and waxes. Some leads contain plastic, which acts as a graphite binding agent.[35] Graphite is a crystalline material and carbon is amorphous. Clays are fine-grained deposits primarily composed of aluminum and/or magnesium. Waxes are primarily esters of fatty acids and other saturated hydrocarbons.

One pencil "lead" formulation patented in 1989 is made up primarily of 15 to 70% graphite powder and finely ground fire clay, in the amount of 3 to 60%. The graphite preparation includes use of 0.1 to 20% digestion agent, which may be alkali phosphate, alkali borate, or alkali carbonate, plus a combination of carbon black, up to 35% and water 3.0 to 50%.[36]

Analysis of pencil lines on paper for the purpose of identifying the manufacturer of the pencil or differentiating written lines has proven to be wrought with difficulties. As Harrison points out, "the greater the proportion of graphite in the lead, the darker is the line which is made with a fixed pressure.[37] "Fixed pressure" is difficult to quantify—as it is function of the force applied to the pencil—and the sharpness of the pencil.

The wax component of the written pencil line has been analyzed by thin layer chromatography, but this procedure did not prove to be sensitive enough to provide a means of differentiation.[38] Binders present in pencil have been analyzed by GC-MS.[39] Yablokov stated in 1995 that electrical resistance of pencil lines on paper is increased with hardness (higher graphite content). However, pencils of close hardness number exhibit insignificant conductivity differences and the aforementioned writing pressure can greatly influence total lead (graphite) deposition.[40] Pencil lead analysis will continue to be an area of forensic research. An industry source for current information about pencils and pencil lead composition is the Writing Instrument Manufacturers Association.

Photocopier Toners

Another non-ink material you may be asked to chemically analyze is toner. Photocopier and laser printer toners typically consist of resins; cross-linking agents (compounds having two or more double bonds capable of polymerizing); binding agents; carriers; various additives and, with color laser copiers/printers, coloring agents. Ingredients such as dispersants and solvents evaporate rapidly. Other ingredients may be present; however, the following are some specific examples of substances that can potentially be detected in toner.

Color Copier/Printer Toner

This toner[41] was introduced in 1999.

BINDER RESIN. Polystyrene; styrene derivative homopolymers such as poly-p-chlorostyrene and polyvinyl toluene; styrene copolymers such as styrene-p-chlorostyrene copolymers, styrene-vinyl toluene copolymers, styrene-vinyl naphthalene copolymers, styrene-ester acrylate copolymers, styrene-ester methacrylate copolymers, styrene-a-methyl chloromethacrylate copolymers, styrene-acrylonitrile copolymers, styrene-vinylmethylether copolymers, styrene-vinylethylether copolymers, styrene-vinylmethylketone copolymers, styrene-butadiene copolymers, styrene-isoprene copolymers, styrene-acrylonitrile-indenecopolymers; polyvinyl chloride; phenol resin; naturally denaturated phenol resin; naturally denaturated maleic acid resin; acrylic resin; methacrylic resin; polyvinyl acetate; silicone resin; polyester resin; polyurethane; polyamide resin; furan resin; epoxy resin; xylene resin; polyvinyl butyral; terpene resin; coumarone-indene resin; and petroleum resin.

Toner parent particles are formed from polymerizing monomers from among the following: Styrenes and their derivatives such as styrene, poly-p-chlorostyrene, and polyvinyl toluene; double-bonded monocarboxylic acid and derivatives thereof such as acrylic acid, methyl acrylate, ethyl acrylate, butyl acrylate, dodecyl acrylate, octyl acrylate, acrylic acid-2-ethylhexyl, phenyl acrylate, methacrylic acid, methyl methacrylate, ethyl methacrylate, butyl methacrylate, octyl methacrylate, acrylonitrile, methacrylonitrile, and acrylamide; double-bonded dicarboxylic acid and derivatives thereof such as maleic acid, butyl maleate, methyl maleate, and dimethyl maleate; vinyl esters such as vinyl chloride, vinyl acetate, and vinyl benzoate; ethylene olefins such as ethylene, propylene, and butylene; vinyl ketones such as vinylmethyl ketone and vinylhexyl ketone; and vinyl ethers such as vinylmethyl ether, vinylethyl ether, and vinyl isobutyl ether.

Cross-linking polymers are formed from among the following: Aromatic divinyl compounds such as divinyl benzene and divinyl naphthalene; carboxylic acid ester having two double bonds such as ethylene glycol diacrylate, ethylene glycol dimethacrylate, and 1,3-butanediol dimethacrylate; divinyl compounds such as divinyl aniline, divinyl ether, divinyl sulfide, and divinyl sulfone (Fig. 3.25); and compounds with three or more vinyl groups.

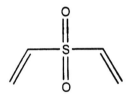

Figure 3.25. Divinyl sulfone.

Divinyl sulfone Chemical Data

- Empirical formula: $C_4H_6O_2S$
- Molecular weight: 118.1502

MAGNETIC MATERIALS. Iron oxides such as magnetite, hematite, and ferrite; magnetic metals such as iron, cobalt, and nickel; and alloys of these with non-magnetic metals such as aluminum, cobalt, copper, lead, magnesium, tin, zinc, antimony, beryllium, bismuth, cadmium, calcium, manganese, selenium, titanium, tungsten, vanadium, and mixtures thereof.

SURFACE TREATING AGENTS. Silane coupling agents and titanium coupling agents.

SURFACE ACTIVE AGENTS. Sodium dodecyl sulfate, sodium tetradecyl sulfate, sodium pentadecyl sulfate, sodium octyl sulfate, sodium oleate, sodium laurate, potassium stearate, calcium oleate, and mixtures thereof.

CHARGE CONTROLLING AGENTS. Organometallic compounds such as organometallic complexes or chelate compounds of aromatic hydroxycarboxy acids such as salicylic acid, alkylsalicylic acid, dialkylsalicylic acid, naphthoic acid, and dicarboxylic acid. Other examples include sulfonic acid, polymer-type compounds with carboxylic acid as side chains, boron compounds, carbamide compounds, silicone compounds, and calixarenes. Examples of positive charge controlling agents include: quaternary ammonium salts, polymer-type compounds with the quaternary ammonium salts as side chains, guanidine compounds, and imidazole compounds. The charge controlling agents are preferably included in the toner parent particles at a ratio of 0.5 to 10 parts by weight per 100 parts by weight of binder resin.

FLOWABILITY IMPROVING AGENTS. Inorganic oxides (silicon oxide, aluminum oxide, and titanium oxide), carbon black, and carbon fluoride. Preferably, these have been subjected to hydrophobic treatment.

POLISHING AGENTS. Metal oxides (strontium titanate, ceric oxide, aluminum oxide, magnesium oxide, and chromium oxide), nitrides (silicon nitride), carbides (silicon carbide), and metal salts (calcium sulfate, barium sulfate, and calcium carbonate). Suitably used lubricants include fluorine resin powders (polyvinylidene fluoride and polytetrafluoroethylene) and fatty acid metal salts (zinc stearate and calcium stearate).

Metal oxides (tin oxide, titanium oxide, zinc oxide, silicon oxide, and aluminum oxide) and carbon black. These additives are preferably used within a range of 0.1 to 10 parts by weight to 100 parts by weight of toner parent particles, and more preferably used within a range of 0.1 to 5 parts by weight.

COLORING AGENTS.
- Black: Carbon black.
- Yellow: Isoindolinone compounds, anthraquinone compounds, azo metal complexes, methine compounds, arylamide compounds. Examples include C. I. Pigment Yellow 12, 13, 14, 15, 17, 62, 74, 83, 93, 94, 95, 97, 109, 110, 111, 120, 127, 128, 129, 147, 168, 174, 176, 180, 181, and 191.

- Magenta: Condensation azo compounds, diketopyrrolopyrrole compounds, anthraquinone compounds, quinacridone compounds, base dye lake compounds, naphthol compounds, benzimidazolone compounds, thioindigo compounds, and perylene compounds. Specific examples include C. I. Pigment Red 2, 3, 5, 6, 7, and 23.
- Cyan: Copper phthalocyanine compounds and derivatives, anthraquinones, base dye lake compounds, e.g., C. I. Pigment Blue 1, 7, and 15.

A procedure for analyzing toner by diffuse reflectance infrared spectroscopy is described in Chapter 6. Toners have also been analyzed using pyrolysis gas chromatography/mass spectrometry, and scanning electron microscopy-energy dispersive x-ray microanalysis (SEM-EDX).[42]

Ink Chemistry Resources

To protect trade secrets, manufacturers are generally reluctant to disclose specific ingredients in their inks. However, the U.S. Patent and Trademark Office offers a vast resource of information on ink composition. You can now access all inks covered by un-expired U.S. Patents–on the Internet. Search by either the Boolean method or patent number. The current Internet starting point for both is www.uspto.gov/patft/index.html. Examine the patented ingredient lists and you will see specific compounds which may be present in the inks you are analyzing and you will see the magnitude of the problem of exhaustive chemical characterization of inks in forensic analyses. You will also find chemical information on some dyes found in writing pen inks (some of which are also used as biological staining reagents). And you can find additional information about dyes and pigments from the *Textile Chemist and Colorist & American Dyestuff Reporter* (ISSN 1526-2847) of the American Association of Textile Chemists and Colorists or the British organization, Society of Dyers and Colourists. For detailed technical information, you can consult the journal *Dyes and Pigments* (ISSN: 0143-7208) that covers the scientific and technical aspects of the chemistry and physics of dyes, pigments, and their intermediates. Information on dyes, pigments, and most industrial substances is also available in *The Encyclopedia of Chemical Technology* (John Wiley and Sons, Publisher, ISBN 047152688-6) and *Ullman's*

Encyclopedia of Industrial Chemistry (ISBN 0-89573-159-2), available in most college chemistry libraries.

Many software and Internet resources are available for chemical data. One such recommendable website currently available is *www. chemfinder.com.*

REFERENCES

1. www.Chemfinder.com.
2. Waring, D. R. & Hallas, G.: *The Chemistry and Application of Dyes,* 1990, pp. 238–239.
3. www.colour-index.org/intro.asp.
4. Fabien, B.: Formulabs, personal conversation, September 18, 2001.
5. Daugherty, P. M.: Director of Chemical Research, Scripto, Inc. Atlanta, Ga. Unpublished paper: Composition of Ball Pen Inks.
6. Peters, A. T. & Freeman, H. S.: *Physico-Chemical Principles of Color Chemistry,* Vol. 4, 1996, p. 202.
7. Ibid., p.229.
8. Ibid., p. 203.
9. Ibid., p. 211.
10. Ibid., p. 218.
11. Andrasko, J.: HPLC Analysis of ballpoint pen inks stored at different light conditions. *JFS* 2001; 46(1), pp. 21–30.
12. Waring, D. R. & Hallas, G.: *The Chemistry and Application of Dyes,* 1990, p. 42.
13. Laden, P.: *Chemistry and Technology of Water Based Inks,* 1997, p. 113.
14. Paulin, P.: Regulatory Chemist, Sanford Corporation. Personal correspondence, May 26, 2000.
15. United States Patent 4,077,807.
16. United States Patent 5,314,531.
17. United States Patent 5,942,027.
18. United States Patent 5,314,531.
19. United States Patent 5,942,027.
20. United States Patent 5,942,027.
21. United States Patent 5,314,531.
22. United States Patent: 6,004,388.
23. United States Patent 5,993,098.
24. United States Patent: 5,712,328.
25. United States Patent 5,466,281.
26. United States Patent 5,961,703.
27. United States Patent 6,054,505.
28. Flynn, W.: *Newsletter of American Board of Forensic Document Examiners,* p. 23, Nov. 26, 1995.
29. Doherty, P.: Classification of ink jet printers and inks. *Journal of the American*

Society of Questioned Document Examiners, 1/2: 88–96, December, 1998.

30. Solodar, W: Designing dyes for ink jet inks. *Int. J. Forensic Document Examiners*, 4/1: 22–24, Jan/Mar, 1998.
31. United States Patent: 4,329,262.
32. Sheaffer Pen Corporation: *Technical Sheet A–Script Fountain Pen Ink*, 2000.
33. Throckmorton, G.: Disappearing ink: Its use, abuse, and detection, *JFS*, 35/1, pp. 199–203, January, 1990.
34. *Bank Security Devices.* FBI Chemistry Unit Publication.
35. Witz, W.: Kohinoor Corporation, Personal conversation with author; April 20, 1998.
36. United States Patent 5,118,345.
37. Harrison, W.: *Suspect Documents*, p. 25, 1958.
38. Cain, S., Cantu, A. A., Brunelle, R., & Lyter, A.: A Scientific Study of Pencil Lead Components. *JFS*, February, 1978.
39. Zoro, J. A. & Totty, R. N.: The application of mass spectrometry to the study of pencil marks. *JFS*, 25: 675-678, 1980.
40. Yablokov, N. P.: Criminal investigation of materials of documents. *Int. J. Forensic Document Examiners*, 1/2:121–267, April/June, 1995.
41. United States Patent: 6,106,990.
42. Brandi, J., James, B., & Gutowski, S. J.: Differentiation and classification of photocopier toners; *Int. J. Forensic Document Examiners.*

Chapter 4

PRELIMINARY METHODS OF INK ANALYSIS

INTRODUCTION

By *preliminary methods of ink analysis*, we mean those methods that you can learn and perform relatively quickly and that do not involve instrumental chemical analysis. Microscopic examination reveals pen type and permits preliminary color assessment of the pen line. Laser irradiation is used to excite luminescence. With video spectral analysis, we examine UV-VIS-NIR responses. There are also newly described computerized digital image processing techniques that show promise as inexpensive methods of ink differentiation. With the exception of video spectral equipment and laboratory-grade lasers, all equipment required for these procedures is relatively inexpensive.

PEN LINE MICROSCOPY

Identification of the type of ink can tell you the general chemical composition of an ink, and which technique is likely to be successful for differentiation and identification of the ink in question. It also provides the first means of assessing whether two samples could have been produced with the same pen or could have had the same origin. Stereo microscopy (ca. 10X to 60X) with reflected fiber optic illumination will normally reveal the features of a pen line that tell you what kind of writing instrument (or other device) was used to make it. Use the following guideline to identify the ink's source from its microscopic appearance; however, you will need known-source standards for casework. This list is not exhaustive of inks or application methods.

Microscopic Features of Ink and Related Substances

Writing Pens

BALLPOINT PEN INK. Writing groove almost always present. Striations may be present. Gooping also common, especially when striations are present. No fiber diffusion or shading.

WRITING GROOVE. Depression or furrow of the line into the paper made by a ball-type pen (visible with oblique lighting).

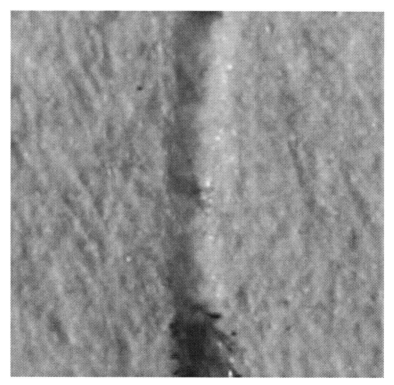

Figure 4.1. Writing groove (40x).

STRIATIONS. These are fine uninked streaks within the ink line of a width, usually no more than about one-fifth that of the ink line. In ballpoint pens, they are caused by contamination on the ball or burrs on the ball casing which remove ink from the ball as the latter rotates in the casing. Ballpoint pen striations extend from inside to outside of a pen line curve in the direction of pen movement. In fiber-tipped pens, splitting of fiber bundles causes striations.

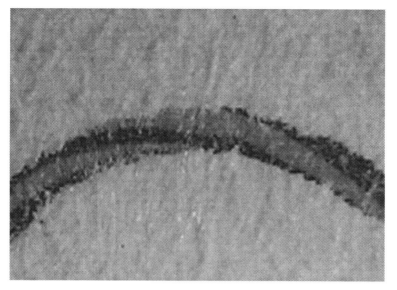

Figure 4.2. Ballpoint striations (40x).

GOOPING. Also called globbing, heavy depositions of ink at spots along the ink line.

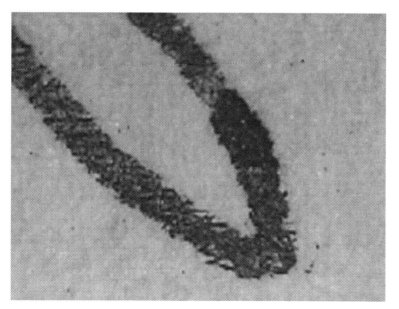

Figure 4.3. Ballpoint gooping (40x).

FIBER DIFFUSION. This is diffusion of ink from the ink line into and between adjacent paper fibers. It is characteristic of water-based inks.

ROLLER-BALL PEN INK. Writing groove almost always present, although usually more shallow than that of ballpoint. Usually no striations or gooping. Fiber diffusion may be present.

FIBER-TIPPED PEN INK. The stylus, which is made up of compressible fibers, is of insufficient hardness to produce a writing groove, as seen in a ballpoint pen line. The ink is usually water-based in ordinary writing pens; so fiber-diffusion may be present. Fibers of stylus bundle may split, forming wide striations within ink line. Individual or small groups of fibers may fray with use and produce fine lines alongside main ink line.

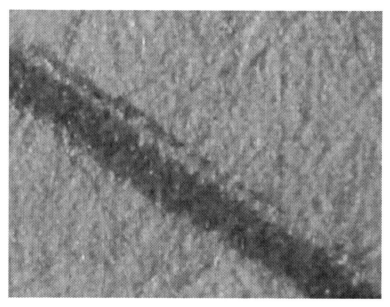

Figure 4.4. Fiber-tip pen striation/fiber bundle split (40x).

FELT-TIPPED PEN INK. Stylus may be a soft or compressed, non-abrasive material, neither of sufficient hardness to produce writing groove. It is more commonly used for coarse markers. Ink may be organic solvent or water-based, the latter potentially exhibiting paper fiber diffusion.

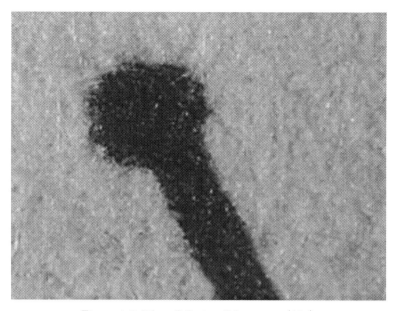

Figure 4.5. Fiber diffusion/felt-tip pen (40x).

FOUNTAIN PEN INK. Pen is nib point, thus dual tracks (nib marks) may be present, depending upon the nib hardness, tip roundedness, and pressure applied. This consumer-filled pen normally contains water-based ink, which leads to paper fiber diffusion. A distinctive characteristic among hard-tipped fountain pens is "shading" of stroke. This is substantial variation in the width of the ink line, in regions of approximately equal pen point pressure as pen nibs separate. Shading is usually seen with up and down strokes. Pen line usually narrows when pen moves horizontally. (Shading may also be seen in beveled fiber tipped pens sold for calligraphy.) Fountain pen ink lines may exhibit "flow-back" of ink, at the end of written lines, causing a darkening of the line end. The latter feature may be present in writing made with calligraphic felt-tipped pens or with gel ink pens (see below).

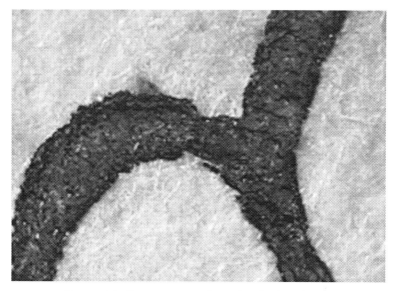

Figure 4.6. Fountain pen nib tracks/shading (40x).

POROUS-TIP PEN INK. Featuring a hard stylus with opening in tip, it normally uses water-based ink. Writing groove and fiber diffusion may be present.

GEL-PEN INK. Pen uses a ball and casing similar to ballpoint or roller ball. Chemically, it is a different type ink than either (as discussed in Chapter 3). The ink line is unlikely to exhibit gooping or striations. Lines are dark and stable with vivid color. Writing groove may be pre-

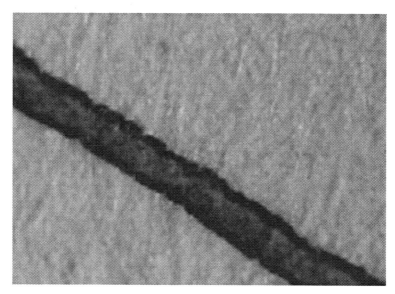

Figure 4.7. Gel-pen ink line (40x).

sent; however, the pen writes so smoothly that many writers reduce pen point pressure, minimizing groove. Even in the absence of a pen defect, heavy writing pressure often leaves a lightly inked center portion in the ink line, similar to that of a fountain pen. Microscopic examination reveals a single ball track rather than dual nib tracks, and gel ink is easily distinguished from fountain pen ink.

Non-Pen Inks and Related Substances

These inks, found in font or graphic images, can also be distinguished by microscopic features. In addition, the macroscopic appearance and use on the document is usually a clue to the ink's origin.

TYPEWRITER INK. Cloth-ribbon typewriter ink is deposited by an impact-device, e.g., type font or dot matrix printer pin. Font typewriter ink impressions are microscopically distinguished from "carbon" ribbon impressions by their comparatively dull and less well-defined edges. Dot matrix impressions are formed by impacted ink dots of a number of degrees of density and image sharpness. By contrast, carbon ribbon impressions exhibit microscopic edge fractures and paper fiber impressions. This enables document examiners to identify the very ribbon used to produce the impression.

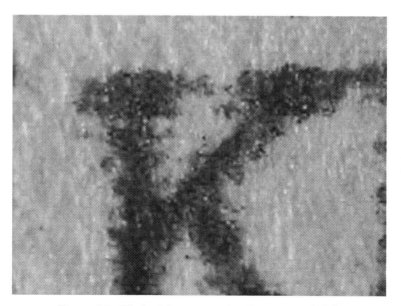

Figure 4.8. Cloth ribbon typewriter impression (40x).

RUBBER STAMP INK. Typically black or red ink, this ink is usually recognizable in context, e.g., imperfectly aligned signature, number or notation on a document. A rubber or polymer plastic printing surface deposits the ink. Indentation is unlikely. The mat surface may inadvertently ink surrounding area.

OFFSET PRINTING INK. Mass-produced, high-quality printing material, offset ink may be any color. Microscopically, it is distinguished from copier or printer origin by sharp edges and a lack of toner spatter. Portions may be produced with "screening," i.e., evenly spaced dots.

Figure 4.9. Offset printing (40x).

INK JET PRINTER INK. Product may be black or may contain multicolored images. Ink is propelled onto paper to form irregularly shaped dots that are visible microscopically. Some color spatter may be present around image areas but not all over the page as with toner products. Some paper fiber diffusion may be seen, especially on uncoated paper. Because of fiber diffusion, high-resolution printers can print images of handwriting from graphics files that resemble original handwriting performed with a liquid-ink pen.[1]

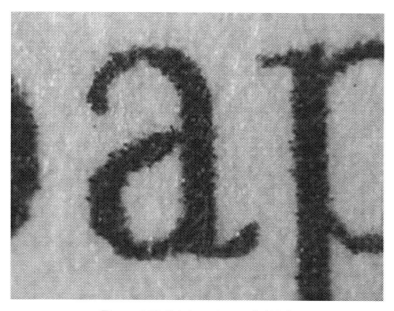

Figure 4.10. Ink jet printer ink (40x).

LETTERPRESS INK. This ink is impressed onto paper from a raised surface, producing an image similar to a type font impression. A darkened halo may be present around edge of image. It is usually used for sequential numbering.

COPIER/LASER PRINTER TONER. Image is formed from heat-fused resin-coated pigments on paper surface. Spatter across all paper surface may be present. Dry toner forms discrete granules; liquid toner appears to dye the paper fibers.[2] On color printers and copiers, large solid color areas can exhibit microscopic streaks.

DYE PACK. "Dye pack" is a stain used to mark stolen currency by incorporation into an exploding device. It is usually seen as a red ink-like spatter on suspect currency.

PENCIL. Pencil lines are usually recognizable with the unaided eye; however, without microscopic examination, some may be mistaken for black pen lines. Microscopically, pencil "lead" will pile against paper fibers on the side opposite the direction of pencil movement. Under magnification, pencil lead, which is actually a combination of graphite, clays, and other assorted materials, is usually unmistakable with its scattered particles and glisten (spectral reflectance).

INK COLOR ASSESSMENT

It is often a color difference between the ink of a questioned entry and other writing on a page which initially draws attention to the questioned entry as a possible addition or alteration to a document. Visual color assessment is one of the first steps to take after you have determined that two ink samples were produced with the same type of writing instrument or other device. There are three elements that contribute to subjective color assessment—sample, light source, and observer. As discussed in Chapter 3, an ink sample, by virtue of the structure of its composite colorants, generates color by selective absorption of visible light.

Primary Colors of Light and of Colorants

Red, green, and blue are the primary colors of light. A mix of light sources of these colors will produce the other colors of light. Colorants, such as ink dyes and pigments, are substances that selectively absorb wavelengths of light and it is the reflected light that you perceive as color. The primary colors of colorants, red, yellow, and blue, can be mixed in various combinations to produce other desired colors. When viewing dyes and pigments, the colors that you see may be the actual reflected colors—or they may be additive colors produced by addition of different reflected colors.

Arbitrary Color Notation

One simple method of recording color differences and similarities of inks is to assign your own designations beginning with the first ink you examine in a particular case. For instance, if you examine a blue ink sample and call its color "blue 1" and then you compare it with another blue ink, which has a slightly different hue, you can call the second color "blue 2." If the third sample matches the first, record that the color of the third ink as "blue 1." This method obviates the additional and indirect step of correctly classifying the colors of the samples using a standardized color notation system. Just be sure to make a note to yourself in your worksheet that this is what you mean by these designations.

Color Assessment of Black Inks

With the unaided eye, most entries written with black ballpoint pens appear indistinguishable. Microscopically, their differences may be striking. To see this, collect several brands of black ballpoint pens, draw close parallel lines on a sheet of paper, and compare the lines' macroscopic and microscopic appearance. Microscopic examination of black ink lines often reveals that some black inks have a slightly purple hue. This distinction may not be perceptible without juxtaposing the line with a pure black color sample (Munsell notation N0/) or another pen line that is pure black.

Color Perception

Accurate visual color assessment of inks requires that you take into account a number of possible limitations that relate to human color perception. Light-sensitive cells in the retina include rods and cones. Rods contain a pigment with a maximum sensitivity at approximately 510 nm (green). However, while they permit low-light or scotopic vision, that vision is entirely monochromatic. The human eye can distinguish millions of colors, and this discrimination is based upon selective stimulation of cones, the color-resolving light-sensitive cells in our eyes. Cones are divided among those that are sensitive to light of different regions of the visible spectrum; thus, there are short (S), middle (M), and long-wavelength sensitive (L) cones. These are more commonly known as blue, green, and red cones. This is actually a misnomer, since some wavelengths that stimulate one type of cone may create the sensation of a combination of these colors. Neitz and Jacobs have indicated possibly a forth type of cone in the human retina.[3] For the present purposes, we will disregard this complication.

Color is the subjective perception of the combination of light wavelengths which reach the retina, and which trigger nerve impulses to the brain. The perception of an ink line as being a specific color occurs when the ink absorbs electromagnetic radiation in the human visible range. If the ink absorbs no electromagnetic radiation in the human visible range, it will appear white. If it absorbs all light of the human visible spectrum, it will appear black. If the ink absorbs one region of the visible spectrum, it will be seen as the complementary color. For instance, if an ink absorbs red light, then the ink will appear blue-green.

The human visible spectrum is usually stated as 400 nm–700 nm, although a more precise measure for normal vision is 380–730 nm. The shorter wavelength is bounded by the ultraviolet and the longer by the infrared. The exact wavelength limits for the "visible spectrum" are stated slightly differently in different references, sometimes to round off the figure. Also, from a physiological standpoint, the limits of the human visual spectrum are inexact because people vary in their ability to see at wavelengths beyond the normal visible region. Some people can see slightly into the ultraviolet and into the infrared.[4]

Factors Contributing to Color Perception Variation

PHYSIOLOGICAL. Color vision deficiencies occur in about 7%–8% of males and 0.4% of females.[5] An absence of cones, a condition in which the person sees only with rods ("rod-monochromacy"), is true color-blindness. If you perform forensic color comparisons, be aware of any deficiencies you have. Presumptive color perception tests are available on the Internet. An optometrist or ophthalmologist can provide a more in-depth test if necessary.

BACKGROUND EFFECT. Colors adjacent to a sample under observation may also affect perception of the color of the sample. In the case of inks, this usually means the color of the paper. Control for this when contrasting and comparing ink lines.

ILLUMINATION. You can define any illumination source by its spectral power distribution curve–the function of electromagnetic power vs. wavelength. The choice of illumination may affect color perception independently of any visual deficiencies of the observer. So long as you illuminate an object with white light, you will generally see it as the same color under different light sources. The exception occurs in the case of metamers, objects that are perceived as the same color under one white light but appear to be a different color under another white light source.

In speaking of a single sample, *color constancy* is the tendency of a sample to appear approximately the same color under sunlight and under artificial light illumination. Some inks may lack color constancy and some pairs of inks may be metamers of each other. The same may be true of separated dyes in a thin layer chromatogram.

Because of lack of color constancy of some samples and the possibility of metamers, color analysis generally requires examination under two sources of illumination—a common interior light source and natural or simulated sunlight.

Color Notation

Because technical color assessment requires standardized terminology, scientists have developed several color notation and color space systems. Each system has its advantages and disadvantages, depending upon the application. Understanding color notation and color space will generally provide the analyst with an understanding of the parameters in which the colors of objects may be compared. The subject is worth reviewing in preparation for visual color comparison.

COLOR SPACE AND COLOR NOTATION. The following systems can be used for producing objective reference material denoting color samples. These systems, however, are most useful in ink analysis through computerized interpretation of reflectance spectra using microspectrophotometry, a technique that is discussed in more detail in Chapter 6. Spectrophotometer software is available for Munsell, CIE, and Tristimulus.[6]

Munsell Notation, which assigns designations for hue, value, and chroma, places colors into a three-dimensional chart called the Munsell Color Space. These terms are used as follows:
- Hue (H): Named attribute of color as green, red, etc.
- Value (V): Lightness/brightness, i.e., dark to light.
- Chroma (C): Colorfulness or departure from "true" color, e.g., "reddish-brown" vs. "red."

These attributes are written in "Munsell notation" as "H V/C." *Hue* is identified by a number from 1–100 or, alternatively, by its sector on the Munsell Hue Circles—and a number of 1–10.

As an example, "5R" is a designation in the middle of the red sector. Adding numerical values for value and *chroma*, a sample might have a Munsell notation of 5R 6/14.

Value ranges from 0 for pure black, to 10 for white.

The chroma scale ranges from 0 for neutral colors (gray-scale) to an indeterminate end. The extension of the chroma attribute on this scale varies with the material. Highly reflecting materials may extend to 20, fluorescent materials to 30.

Three-dimensional charts for this color classification system are the Munsell color space and Munsell color solid.

Details on Munsell are available in the *American Society for Testing and Materials* (ASTM) publication D 1535, *Test Method of Specifying Color by the Munsell System.*

One use of Munsell notation for ink analysis is to record the macroscopic/microscopic visual color assessment by reference to standardized color charts. One such chart, the Munsell Color Order System (*Munsell Book of Color*), is useful for color description of ink lines (*in situ*) and for color description of TLC bands.

Another set of color nomenclature specifically designed for dyes is the *Color Index Hues*, which is published by Colour Index International.

A color classification system commonly used throughout industry and in forensic science is published by the Commission Internationale de l'Eclairage, or CIE (French for "International Commission on Illumination"). This commission publishes the CIELAB system, with its "CIELAB color space" which represents color from a combination of three axes: x, y, and z, where x represents the amount of redness in a colors, y the amount of greenness and lightness (bright-to-dark), and z the amount of blueness. The CIE method assumes a standard observer and daylight illuminant.

A difference in colors of two samples in a CIELAB model is designated Delta E (delta, meaning "difference," and "E" from the German "Empfindung" for "sensation"). The superscript asterisk is also used to denote a CIELAB difference, as in "DE*".

A refinement, the 1976 (L*a*b) color space uses an L* axis for lightness (0 = black, 100 = white); a* for Red-greeness and b* for yellow-blueness. When a* = b*, the sample is colorless and the L* axis simply measures the sample along a gray-scale. The 1976 (L*a*b) color space maps the distances between color coordinates in a manner that closely resembles human color perception. Depending upon which color space you use, the distance between color coordinates may or may not represent differences which are perceptible to the human eye. This correlation is of more interest to industry color analysts than to forensic scientists. Our goal is to determine whether two inks are different or possibly the same chemical composition–as indicated by their color. Any available system which may reveal color differences–whether visible or not–serves our purpose.

Most visible colors can be created by a combination of red, green, and blue, the three "primary" colors. The remaining visible colors can be created theoretically by adding two primaries and subtracting the other one. A color-coding system based upon the three types of human cones produces a tristimulus value for a color, i.e., a three-variable (X, Y, Z) formula created by specifying the amounts of Red (X), Green (Y), and Blue (Z) to match the sample in question. Each wavelength in the visible range has a specific tristimulus value, e.g., 500 nm has values $X = 0.0049$, $Y = 0.3230$ and $Y = 0.2720$.

To provide a two-dimensional plot of color which correlates better with human visual perception, CIE recommended in 1931 that tristimulus values be converted to chromaticity coordinates, x, y, and z by the formulas:

$$x = X/(X + Y + Z)$$
$$y = Y/(X + Y + Z)$$
$$z = Z/(X + Y + Z)$$

Since three chromaticity coordinates add up to 1, only two need be specified for a color. The chromaticity diagram (x vs. y) is two-dimensional. A graph of x and y is called a chromaticity diagram. Add a third dimension Y, to represent lightness, and you have the CIE Y, x, y diagram.

COLOR AND TLC. Manufacturers include some colorants to reflect the principle color of the ink line. Blue or black dyes, as well as some dyes which are magenta, cyan, or yellow, are used to absorb colors. By this method, a desired hue is achieved through color mixing. These different colored ingredients can be seen once they are separated. For instance, while a written ink line is typically blue or black–the separated pure components on a chromatographic plate may provide a wide array of colors for comparison, many of which are completely unlike that of the whole ink. Color assessment may be even more useful after thin layer chromatographic separation of the ink dye components.

The same compound/band in different TLC's may have the same Hue and Chroma, but the "Value" in Munsell notation of two equivalent bands may vary with concentration. A TLC scanning densitometer can objectively assess this difference, as a measure of optical density.

INTERDISCIPLINARY COORDINATION FOR COLOR ASSESSMENT. As mentioned in Chapter 2, the ink analyst may benefit from the coordination of training and equipment used with other specialized crime laboratory sections. Color analysis, both visual and instrumentally measured, is used extensively in forensic paint and fiber analysis as well as characterization of inks. An ink analyst of a crime laboratory may find it useful to work with the trace evidence section to develop methods of color assessment and characterization.

RESOURCES ON COLOR THEORY. Many resources on color theory are available on the World Wide Web. These resources can be searched via technical terms or the names of the following organizations:

- American National Standards Institute
- Inter-Society Color Council
- International Commission on Illumination (CIE)
- International Color Consortium
- International Organization for Standardization
- Optical Society of America
- Society of Dyers and Colourists
- University of Leeds, Department of Colour Chemistry
- Laboratory of Color Information
- Munsell Color Science Laboratory
- Color and Vision Research Laboratories, San Diego

MICROSCOPIC SPECULAR REFLECTANCE

Of the light striking an ink sample, some will be absorbed, a small amount may be transmitted and the rest will be "reflected." Reflection occurs when light strikes a boundary at which there is a change in refractive index between air and the reflecting ink. This causes the light to travel in the original medium (air) with a change in direction. Reflectance is quantified as the proportion of electromagnetic radiation which is reflected by a surface, measured from total reflectance = 1, to no reflectance = 0.

Specular reflectance is reflectance of all light in one direction, viz., the opposite angle to the incident light–as in a mirror. Diffuse reflectance is reflectance of light in different directions, caused by surface irregularities, and is used in instrumental analyses, such as infrared spectroscopy. The nature of the ink surface will determine the reflectance characteristics, including the angle of incident light that produces specular reflectance. You can use the specular aspect as a screening test for ink differentiation.

Procedure

Microscopically examine the compared ink lines with reflected oblique fiber-optic illumination.
- Vary the angle of illumination and note whether the ink exhibits specular reflectance (seen as a glare or glisten) and at what angle this specular reflectance occurs.
- Compare and record this effect for all ink samples on the same document.
- If the inks exhibit the same specular reflectance, then their surface characteristics are similar and you have evidence that they may be the same formulation. If two inks do not exhibit the same specular reflectance characteristics, you have presumptive evidence that they are not the same formulation.
- Although a microscope and light source are usually adequate for specular reflectance estimates, industry colorists make this measurement with a spectroradiometer.

VIDEO SPECTRAL ANALYSIS

Introduction

Video spectral analysis is performed with equipment that uses a charge couple device (CCD) to acquire an image of a document from a stage. The image is projected onto a monitor. A variety of illumination and filtering devices reveal differences in infrared absorption, transmittance, and luminescence and longwave UV excitation of visible luminescence (fluorescence) of ink.

Video spectral analysis provides one advantage over all other types of ink analyses: It permits a quick examination of the entire questioned document, and may reveal ink differences in context, or similarities in chemical formulation.

Light-Matter Interactions: Terminology

PHOTOLUMINESCENCE. Photoluminescence is the emission of light from a substance due to electromagnetic irradiation and absorption of photons. The two forms are fluorescence and phosphorescence. With fluorescence, there is no change in electron spin and light is re-emitted virtually instantaneously ($<10^{-5}$ s) and continues as long as the irradiation is applied. Fluorescence generally refers to re-emission in the visible region of the spectrum, ca. 400 nm-700 nm. UV Fluorescence (or *UV-excited visible fluorescence*) is used in ink analysis, as is infrared luminescence (or *visible-excited infrared luminescence*). The other photo-luminescence, phosphorescence, in which the re-emission continues after removing the irradiation, may occur during infrared lumines-cence of inks.[7] Chemiluminescence, in contrast to photoluminescence, viz., light emission resulting from chemical reaction, is not known to be used in ink analysis.

COLOR FILTERS. Color filters are filters made of a substrate such as glass, which contain a specific concentration of a light-absorbing chemical, designed to pass a specific waveband of light.

DICHROIC FILTER. A dichroic filter is a filter with transmission peaks at two distinct regions of the electromagnetic spectrum (particularly useful in differentiating inks by infrared luminescence).[8]

INTERFERENCE FILTERS. Recognizable as having a mirror-like sur-face, they are made of multiple dielectric thin films on a substrate such as glass. They use interference to reflect or transmit a narrow wave-length band, including bands in the near-infrared region.

When examining ink samples with a video spectral comparison instrument, you will see infrared absorption differences on the moni-tor as variations in darkness or "shades of gray" of the ink line under examination. If absorption is 100%, the image is black. If absorption is 0% (thus transmittance or reflectance is 100%) the image appears white.

Infrared luminescence appears as bright white, apparently "glow-ing" portions of writing when the writing is illuminated with visible-range light (usually blue-green) using the infrared filter for the wave-length of luminescence of the sample.

Ink analysts also use video spectral instruments to view obliterated images. A wavelength is chosen for detection at which the overlying obliteration exhibits relatively high transmittance, while the underly-ing obliterated images absorb the radiation. This makes the underly-ing writing visible. Also, residue of eradicated ink may be visualized as absorption or luminescence. Such residue may not be visible to the unaided eye.

Current designs of video spectral equipment feature digital image integration. This feature can enhance visualization of weak infrared luminescence (IRL). These instruments also feature optional ultraviolet-visible-near infrared (UV-VIS-NIR) microspectrophotometers and Raman spectrometers.

Modular accessory light sources are available for applications requiring high-intensity, narrow waveband, illumination sources. These are especially useful for luminescence assessment. To facilitate visual comparison of images, split-screen, image overlay and image strobe features are available.

The same examinations for which video spectral devices are used can be performed with an infrared document microscope. This is a low-power microscope with infrared optics coupled to an image converter. These examinations can also be performed using IR photography. However, most laboratories today have discontinued use of such methods in favor of video spectral instruments. These instruments are more versatile, provide instant results, and are easier to use.

Economical Video Spectral Devices

Steven Drexler and Geoffrey Smith[9] have described methods for modifying inexpensive consumer products to fabricate a video spectral system.

Procedure

- Use an infrared camcorder as an IR image converter (cover the IR source on the camera).
- Mount photographic barrier filters on the camera lens.
- Connect the camera to a monitor, or use a video capture device to send the signal to a computer. View and enhance the image with *Adobe Photoshop*®.
- Illuminate the sample with a slide projector or other high-intensity light source. Affix a blue-green Corning filter to the light source for detection of IR luminescence.

Precautions in Video Spectral Analysis

A number of variables can cause inconsistent video spectral responses. These are pen line density variations, contact solvents, and background luminescence.

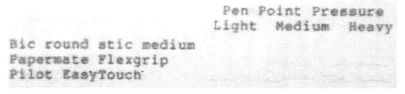

Figure 4.11. Pen lines, visible light.

In Figure 4.11, ink lines drawn with three different brands of black ballpoint pens are indistinguishable to the unaided eye and with visible light microscopy.

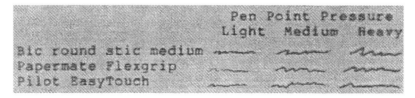

Figure 4.12. Absorption, 830 nm threshold.

In Figure 4.12, all inks exhibit low infrared absorption, and differences are too close to permit differentiation. Notice that the apparent absorption by the sample of the Bic ink written with heavy pen point pressure shows the lowest absorption and appears to be the same absorption as the lowest pen point pressure of the highest absorbing pen, the Pilot ink. Accordingly, when interpreting ink lines of similar absorption, take into account possible ink density variations.

Figure 4.13. Absorption, 600 nm threshold.

The inks in Figure 4.13 cannot be differentiated at this waveband. All of these inks exhibit high absorption.

Figure 4.14. Luminescence, 630 nm threshold.

Figure 4.14 shows luminescence with digital integration, which clearly distinguishes the Bic pen ink line from the other two. This finding eliminates the need for additional testing, if this distinction is the question at issue.

Influences Upon Ink IRL Detection

CONTACT SOLVENTS. Sensi and Cantu[10] reported that contact solvents can affect infrared luminescence. During IRL examination of a signature, they noted that the first name exhibited higher IRL than the surname. Other tests demonstrated that both names were written with ink of the same formulation from a Fisher blue ballpoint pen. This ink contained an IRL component that was masked by other non-IRL components. They theorized that some solvent, possibly perspiration, had come into contact with the first name and caused the IRL component in the first name to be leached out. This accounted for the different responses. They found various degrees of influence upon ink IRL by testing 20 household solvents.

RELATIVE INK/PAPER IRL. Sensi and Cantu also point out that the relative IRL intensity of the paper and the ink can affect visibility of the ink's IRL. If paper IRL is equal to or greater than that of the ink, it will mask IRL of the ink. Similar results in the examination of ink jet printing that were reported by Doherty.[11] Observe this precaution in comparisons of ink IRL between different documents.

PAPER ABSORPTION OF EXCITATION LIGHT. In 1996, Radley[12] found that some colored papers absorbed excitation light. This limited the IRL of the inks on those papers and impeded assessment of the inks' IRL differences. He solved this problem by placing a strongly IRL sheet behind the document under examination, so that the background of the document was brightened. This procedure provided improved differentiation of the inks under examination.

Discrimination of Blue and Black Writing Inks by Video Spectral Analysis

Lloyd Josey, Karen Oroku, and Tracy Tanaka, at the Honolulu Police Crime Laboratory in 2000, reported comparisons of different models of the Foster & Freeman Video Spectral Comparator (VSC) equipment.[13] Their study attempted discriminations of matched pairs of black and blue liquid (water-based) and non-liquid writing inks by microscopy, VSC, Laser, and UV-IR-VIS spectroscopy. (Liquid ink included roller-ball and fiber-tip; non-liquid included ballpoint) The VSC examinations were performed as monitor-assessed video spectral comparisons of IR, IRL, and UV fluorescence responses of the inks.

The older model, VSC-1, successfully discriminated 79.50% of the pairs while the newer VSC-2000 correctly discriminated 95.80%. Of the inks that the older model did not discriminate, some were actually distinguishable by microscopic examination. Use caution when using this instrument for ink comparisons, and don't neglect microscopic color assessment.

LASER-INDUCED FLUORESCENCE (*LIF*) OR LASER-INDUCED INFRARED LUMINESCENCE (*LIRL*) OF INK

A Laser (from *Light Amplification by Stimulated Emission of Radiation*) is a device that produces intense, directional, and coherent electromagnetic radiation. The light emitted from a laser is said to be "lasing" at a single wavelength. Lasers generally permit higher resolution absorption and emission analyses than can be achieved using ordinary light sources in the same spectral range. Currently, lasers are classified as Solid-State, Gas, Dye or Semiconductor. For ink differentiation by laser-induced fluorescence, analysts commonly use Solid-State lasers that incorporate an impurity in glass or crystal, e.g., Nd^{3+} in $Y_3Al_5O_8$, producing an Nd:YAG or "neodymium yttrium aluminum garnet" laser.

Lasers can induce strong luminescence, providing an additional non-destructive technique for ink analysis. In laser-induced fluorescence, the laser fires a pulse into a sample and the light energy is absorbed by the sample. The sample then emits radiation at a longer wavelength. You can focus a laser well within the dimension of a written line.[14] An aberration-corrected microscope objective is needed to achieve the smallest sampling spots. In addition to ink differentiation, you can use lasers to detect chemically eradicated ink.

Laser-induced luminescence has shown mixed results for ink analysis. However, it is worth review because it remains a potential non-destructive means of analysis and most crime laboratories are already equipped with lasers in their Forensic Document and/or Latent Print Sections.

A note of caution: Test any laser prior to casework to determine its likely effect on an evidence sample. Some lasers, especially those used in latent print sections, can destroy ink and paper by photodegradation and heat. In addition, be aware of eye protection requirements of the laser you are using.

PROCEDURE 1. Horton and Nelson[15] used laser-induced infrared luminescence to non-destructively differentiate ballpoint pen inks. They tested 56 pen inks and reported that Nd:YAG laser-induced infrared luminescence (LIRL) could differentiate a significant number of blue (25%) and black (11%) ballpoint pen inks, which could not be differentiated using a non-laser source (tungsten halogen bulb) as an excitation source. This laser-excited luminescence was detected in the 800 nm to 900 nm range, a region not detected by some video spectral devices.

PROCEDURE 2. The same group also used an Nd:YAG source, lasing at 532 nm to differentiate 22 black, eight blue and seven red inks. They successfully differentiated some inks of each category via LIRL; however, there were two important findings in this study.

1. Paper significantly affected LIRL response. Some inks that luminesced on one white paper, did not on another brand.
2. Some LIRL responses changed significantly over six weeks. Control measures must be used to account for both time and background when utilizing this technique.

PROCEDURE 3. Josey et al.[16] (mentioned above for their video spectral studies) conducted comparative studies of black and blue liquid and non-liquid writing inks by laser, video spectral analysis, and visible to near infrared spectroscopy. Laser provided some information, but it was the least effective tool. It discriminated 35% of black liquid pairs, 63% of blue liquid, and 30% of blue non-liquid pairs. It was almost ineffective with black non-liquid, discriminating just 2 of 342 pairs.

DIGITAL IMAGING SOFTWARE

In 2000, William Bodziak[17] reported a technique for differentiating writing ink using a conventional flatbed scanner and a desktop computer equipped with the digital imaging software, *Adobe PhotoShop 5.0.*® He color-scanned questioned and known black ballpoint inks and used the software function Hue/Saturation adjustment to create on-screen color differentiation of black inks of different formulations.

Procedure

- Color-scan the document and open in *PhotoShop*®
- Choose selections beginning with menu heading "Image" to "Adjust" to "Hue/Saturation."
- In this window, you can make adjustments of Hue, Saturation, and Lightness, positively or negatively from settings of the original image. In testing the procedure, the authors found that the settings suggested by Bodziak, viz., Hue = 0; Saturation = +90, Lightness = -7 produced the most pronounced differentiation of black ballpoint inks.

We tested this technique and found that it commonly differentiates black ballpoint inks. The effectiveness of this technique is surprising, particularly since we were using relatively inexpensive equipment that was not specifically designed for ink differentiation.

REFERENCES

1. Flynn, W.: *American Board of Forensic Document Examiners Newsletter*, p. 23, Nov. 26, 1995.
2. *Printing Processes Manual*: New Zealand Police Document Examination Section.
3. Neitz, J., Neitz, M. & Jacobs, G. H.: More than three different cone pigments among people with normal color vision. *Vision Research* 33:117–122, 1993.
4. Beeson, S.: Department of Physics and Astronomy, Arizona State University, Tempe: *Visible Color and the Spectrum.*
5. Howard Huges Medical Institute; www.hhmi.org; 2000.
6. www.fosterfreeman.co.uk.
7. Zimmerman, J., & Mooney, D.: Laser examination as an additional nondestructive method of ink differentiation. *JFS* 33/2: 312. March, 1988.
8. Dick, R. M.: A comparative analysis of dichroic filter viewing, reflected infrared and infrared luminescence applied to ink differentiation problems. *JFS* 15/3: 357–363. July, 1970.
9. Drexler, S. G. & Smith, G.: Ink differentiation for the fiscally challenged. Presented at the 53rd Annual Meeting of the American Society of Forensic Sciences, 2001.
10. Sensi, C. A. & Cantu, A. A.: Is infrared luminescence a valid method to differentiate among inks? Presented at the 33rd Annual Meeting of the American Society of Forensic Sciences, 1981.

11. Doherty, P.: Classification of ink jet printers and inks. *Journal of the American Society of Questioned Document Examiners*, 1/2:88–96, December, 1998.

12. Radley, R. W.: Examination of IRL responses of ballpoint pen inks using luminescent backgrounds. *Int. J. Forensic Document Examiners*, 1/2: 151, Ap/Ju 1996.

13. Josey, L., Oroku, K. G. & Tanaka, T.: Honolulu Police Department Crime Laboratory: Measuring the effectiveness of non-destructive examination of inks utilizing macroscopic/microscopic, infrared, infrared luminescence and ultra-violet techniques and instrumentation. Presentaed at the 52nd Annual Meeting of the American Academy of Forensic Sciences, 2000.

14. Laser Science, Inc. A Subsidiary of Thermo Vision 8E Forge Parkway Franklin, MA 02038.

15. Horton, R. A. & Nelson, L. K.: An evaluation of the use of laser-induced infrared luminescence to differentiate writing inks. *JFS*, 36/3: 838–843. May, 1991.

16. See 12 above.

17. Bodziak, W.: Using a flatbed scanner and Adobe PhotoShop software to distinguish black inks. Presented at the meeting of the American Society of Questioned Document Examiners, 2000.

Chapter 5

FORENSIC COMPARISON AND IDENTIFICATION OF WRITING INKS BY THIN LAYER CHROMATOGRAPHY AND DENSITOMETRY

INTRODUCTION

Inks are examined for three reasons: (1) To compare two or more ink entries to determine similarities or differences in inks. This can provide information concerning whether entries have been added or altered; (2) To determine whether two or more entries were written with the same formula and batch of ink. This provides a lead whether certain entries could have been written with the same pen; (3) To date ink entries to determine if documents have been backdated. This chapter deals with the first two reasons for analyzing inks.

INK COMPARISONS

Non-destructive Methods

Before destructive chemical tests are conducted, ink analysts usually perform preliminary non-destructive tests. This is because chemical analysis requires removing ink from the document, which causes minor damage to the paper. As discussed in Chapter 4, these non-destructive tests typically include: (1) a visual and microscopic examination of the writing to determine the color of the ink and the type of pen used; (2) infrared reflectance and luminescence examinations to determine whether the inks reflect or absorb infrared light and whether the inks luminescence; and (3) viewing the inks under long and short wave ultraviolet light to determine if the inks fluoresce under these wavelengths of light.

These preliminary tests can often determine if two or more inks are different. However, if these techniques do not detect any differences in the inks; further chemical analysis is necessary to determine if the inks being compared are really the same formulation of ink. Figures 5.1 and 5.2 show the results of infrared luminescence and infrared reflectance on an altered medical record using a VSC 2000 Video Scanner.

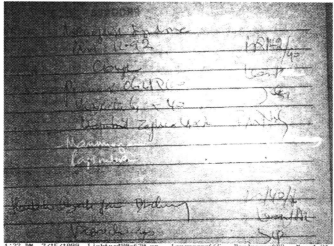

Figure 5.1. Ink differentiation by VSC IR luminescence.

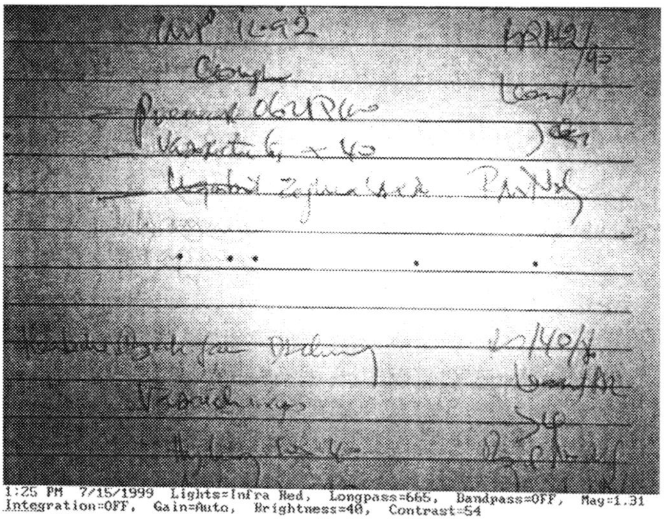

Figure 5.2. Ink differentiation by VSC IR reflectance.

Chemical Methods

The most widely used chemical method for comparing and identifying inks is thin layer chromatography (TLC).[1,2] Chromatography is a chemical technique used to separate the components of a mixture by passing a mobile phase through a stationary phase. The fixed or stationary phase can be a solid or liquid and the mobile phase is either a gas or liquid. Accordingly, chromatography is divided into the categories of gas, liquid, column, paper, and thin layer chromatography. TLC is distinguished from other chromatographic techniques by the use of a thin stationary phase or layer (from 100–250 microns for adsorptive analytical applications) on the surface of a "support," which is a plate of glass, aluminum, or plastic.

The varieties of TLC include adsorption, partition, continuous, stepwise, radial, two-dimensional, forced-flow, and centrifugal. Some of these overlap. Adsorption TLC has been the principle method employed by most labs in forensic ink analysis, although other methods hold promise for future research.

Adsorption TLC (hereafter referred to as "TLC") involves a stationary phase through which a solvent system migrates across the plate by capillary action, separating components of ink samples by interaction of adsorptive forces of the stationary and mobile phases. The different migration rates of the non-volatile components of an ink cause them to separate into "bands."

TLC separates the dyes in the ink as well as the invisible organic components in the ink–which allows a direct comparison of the inks being examined on the same TLC plate. Analysts use TLC densitometry to determine the relative concentrations of the dyes present.

First separate the dyes on the TLC plate using a suitable solvent system.[3] Then, scan the plate using a TLC Scanning Densitometer that measures the relative concentrations of each of the dyes present in the ink. The method is fast, reliable, and inexpensive.

Other chemical methods for examining inks include high-performance liquid chromatography (HPLC)[4,5] electrophoresis,[6,7] gas chromatography[8] and gas chromatography-mass spectrometry (GC-MS).[9] GC and GC-MS are especially useful for measuring volatile components in inks. Unfortunately these volatile components in inks written on paper cannot be detected after a period of six months to one year. Therefore the use of these techniques is limited to inks less than one year old. Another method recently developed for ink comparisons is micellar electrokinetic capillary chromatography (capillary electrophoresis). This method gives excellent separation of dyes used in all types of writing inks and ink jet inks. The resolving power is higher than TLC and HPLC and extremely small sample sizes of 0.5 mm O.D. can give good results.[10]

Tebbett published a comprehensive review of all chromatographic methods used for the forensic comparison of inks.[11] In the early 1990s a standard guide for the comparison and identification of inks was published by ASTM.[12,13] These guides were developed as a cooperative effort by the forensic laboratories of the Unites States Secret Service, the Internal Revenue Service, Brunelle Forensic Laboratories, and others.

Described below is a step-by-step procedure for comparing and identifying inks by TLC and TLC Densitometry. Although this method is not as detailed as the ASTM standard guide, it is sufficient for the great majority of cases. (At the end of this chapter you will find a section on *TLC Theory and Technique* to provide the reader more detailed information on TLC equipment preparation, procedure and quality control, as these relate to ink analysis.)

Equipment, Materials, and Solvents

- Merck HPTLC plates (silica gel without fluorescent indicator). The plates should be activated at 100° C for 15 minutes before use.
- TLC scanning densitometer.
- Reagent grade pyridine, ethyl acetate, 1-butanol, ethanol, benzyl alcohol, dimethyl sulfoxide (DMSO), and water.
- 1 dram glass vials with screw caps.
- 10 µL and 4 µL disposable micropipettes.
- TLC glass developing chamber with cover to accommodate standard 4" x 8" TLC plates.
- 20 gauge syringe needle and plunger (the point of the needle must be filed so that the point is flat).
- 10 µL and 20 µL automatic pipettes.
- Temperature-controlled oven.

Procedure

- Using the syringe needle and plunger, punch out about 10 plugs of ink from the written line.

- Place the plugs in the glass vial and add 1–2 drops of the appropriate solvent to the vial to dissolve the ink (usually pyridine for ballpoint ink and ethanol and water (1:1) for inks other than ballpoint. Water-resistant non-ballpoint inks require using pyridine or DMSO).
- Allow 15 minutes for the ink to dissolve.
- Note and record the color of the ink in solution and then spot the ink on the TLC plate using the 10 µL micropipette. Keep the spots small by spotting intermittently and allowing the spots to dry between each spotting.
- Repeat the above for all inks samples to be compared. Up to 20 samples can be spotted on the same TLC plate. Be sure to analyze a sample of the paper without ink as a control.
- Place the TLC plate with the spotted inks in a temperature-controlled oven for about 10 minutes at 80° C. Then, allow the plate to cool to room temperature. Place the plate in the developing chamber using a solvent system of ethyl acetate, ethanol, and water (70:35:30) respectively. The solvent system should be allowed to equilibrate in the developing chamber for at least 15 minutes.
- Allow the TLC plate to develop 15 minutes, then remove it from the chamber and dry in the oven for 15 minutes at 80° C.
- Examination of an ink thin layer chromatogram (sometimes called *visualization*) routinely involves four parameters: visual, ultraviolet, infrared absorption/reflectance, and infrared luminescence. Spectrophotometric analysis of dye spots may yield additional characterization of the components. Densitometry is usually performed for quantitative analysis.
- View the developed plate visually and under longwave and shortwave ultraviolet light to determine which inks match in terms of dyes and fluorescent components present.

Owing to the nature of the product, writing inks contain a variety of components which when separated by TLC, are immediately visible and, along with their R_f values, are highly characteristic of a specific formulation. (Contrast this to many other organic compounds which when analyzed by TLC often require post-development staining or other visualization treatments, resulting in a chromatogram of one or few distinctive hues.)

Besides visible colors, writing ink components revealed in a thin layer chromatogram often exhibit ultraviolet fluorescence and/or infrared luminescence, providing additional identifying features. Such components may not be visible with the unaided eye. Video spectral analysis is a convenient means of assessing these features, especially IR luminescence (after non-destructive examination of the whole inks, as discussed in the section on video spectral comparison). Video spectral units equipped with digital image integration can detect faint IR luminescence of TLC bands, which, in some cases, may not be visible without this accessory.

Make UV examinations at short wavelength (265 nm) and long wavelength UV (365 nm), preferably using UV viewing cabinets, equipped with irradiation sources for these long and short UV wavelengths. Short wavelength UV will reveal UV absorbing components, while long wavelength UV will excite visible UV fluorescence in certain ink components. Besides standard long wavelength UV lamps, you can use commercially available high-intensity, long wavelength UV lamps to visualize faint UV fluorescence. One such lamp is the Blak-Ray, by UVP, of Upland, California.

Often whole inks, which exhibit no UV fluorescence or IR luminescence, will exhibit one or the other or both in at least one TLC band after TLC development. (Note the parallel between this phenomenon and the effect of contact solvents as described by Sensi and Cantu covered in the section on video spectral analysis, Chapter 4). In addition to its discrimination value in examination of whole inks, IR absorption of the separated components of an ink, in the form of the TLC bands, can be compared using video spectral analysis.

Densitometry

- Scan the plate in the scanning densitometer to measure the relative concentrations of the dyes present in each ink. The dyes are scanned at 585 nm for blue and black inks, if a spectrometer-type densitometer is used. Video densitometers see all spots in shades of black and therefore no wavelength setting is needed for this instrument. For other colored inks, determine the wavelength that provides the maximum absorption by the densitometer and use that wavelength for scanning.
- If the solvent system used did not adequately separate the dyes present in the inks for accurate densitometer readings, repeat the

tests using a solvent system of 1-butanol, ethanol, and water (50:10:15) respectively.

- Compare the relative concentrations of the dyes present in the various inks tested. Failure at this point to detect any significant differences among the inks compared justifies a conclusion that to a high degree of scientific certainty, all inks consist of the same formulation.

This conclusion is based on the finding of no significant differences considering the results of both the non-destructive tests and the chemical analysis.

IDENTIFICATION OF INKS

The same procedures outlined above are used to identify inks, except that standard inks obtained from the manufacturers and from retail stores are required. Before one tries to identify a questioned ink, a comprehensive ink reference collection consisting of most, if not all inks in existence, is required. (Chapter 7 covers development and maintenance of ink libraries.) In addition, considerable experience examining inks is required to be able to distinguish between a batch variation and different formulas of similar inks. To identify the manufacturer and specific formulation of questioned inks, you must compare standard inks of known manufacturer and formulation simultaneous with the questioned inks using the same procedures described above. Figures 5.3 and 5.4 show typical TLC comparisons of a variety of writing inks. Table 5.1 shows the results of an identification of an ink by TLC densitometry.

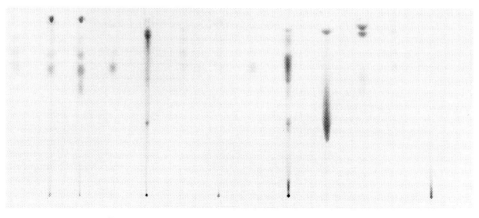

Figure 5.3. Writing ink thin layer chromatograms.

Writing Pen Chromatograms in Figure 5.3 From Left to Right

- Rocket Soft Grip Fine Black Ballpoint
- Black Sharpie Fine Point Black Fiber-tip
- Sharpie Fine Ultra Black Fiber-tip
- Bic USA "Ad" Ballpoint
- Sanford Uni-ball Micro Black Roller-Ball
- Pilot Black Ballpoint Medium
- Rocket Soft Grip Medium Black Ballpoint
- Cross Black Ballpoint Refillable
- Skilcraft Black Fiber-tip
- Skilcraft Red Fiber-tip
- Uni-ball Red Fine Fiber-tip
- Rocket Soft Grip Medium Blue Ballpoint
- Bic Blue Roller-ball
- Paper Control

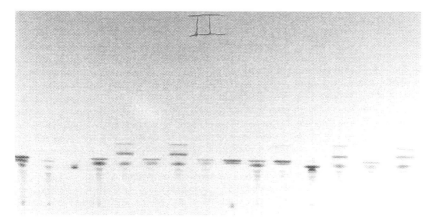

Figure 5.4. Blue ballpoint ink thin layer chromatograms.

Table 5.1
DENSITOMETRIC IDENTIFICATION OF A QUESTIONED INK

Dye	Percent Found (Q Ink)	Papermate Blue Bp
Methyl Violet - 1	35.5	35.6
Methyl Violet - 2	18.8	18.6
Methyl Violet - 3	5.9	6.1
Victoria Blue	39.8	39.7

While the above procedures are the most commonly used and have withstood the test of the courts for the comparison and identification of inks, other methods may sometimes be helpful. For example GC and GC-MS can be used to detect volatile components that might be present in inks.

HPLC can be used to detect volatile and non-volatile components. Electron microscopy can be used to distinguish between carbon and graphite, when these components are present in the inks.

FTIR can be used to differentiate carbonless papers. Figure 5.5 shows that carbonless paper sample b is different than sample a. Sample d is a control sample of carbonless paper. This proved that b had been substituted for the original paper.

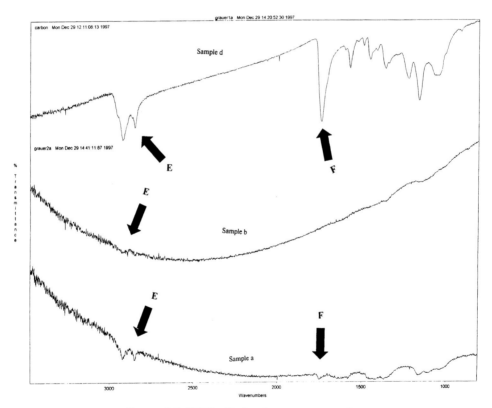

Figure 5.5. FTIR: Carbonless paper samples.

Printing Inks, Artist's Paints, Copier Toners, and Colored Pencils

- Aginsky[14] reported that all of the above substances could be analyzed with TLC.

- First, extract the analyte in dimethylformamide (DMF) using 2-3 microliters, using a one-minute extraction time for a 2 to 3 square mm line of sample.
- If any colored residue remains on the sample after DMF extraction, extract the sample with 2 to 3 microliters of concentrated sulfuric acid for 1 minute.
- Spot the samples on the TLC plate and use three solvent systems on the same samples in succession, i.e., develop in the first solvent system, remove the plate from the developing chamber, dry, and then develop again in the next solvent system, etc.

The solvent systems and development distances for each step are as follows:

- Step 1: 100% Chloroform–Develop 10 cm.
- Step 2: Volume proportions as follows: Ethyl Acetate 30, Isopropanol 15, Water 10, Acetic Acid 1–Develop 7 cm.
- Step 3: Concentrated sulfuric acid–Develop 2 cm.

The authors have not tested this procedure and it should be noted that it does involve use of hazardous reagents. Concentrated acid should only be used with glass-backed plates.

Printing Inks

Jasuja and Sharma[15] successfully analyzed a variety of 20 green, blue, and red offset printing inks with TLC. They cut 5 square millimeter samples of these inks from documents and extracted ink from the paper surface with a few drops of pyridine and glacial acetic acid (3:1).

They found that different color printing inks required different solvent systems.

Printing Ink Color	*Solvent System*
Blue	Chloroform : Methanol : Hexane (8:1:1)
Red	1,2-dichloroethane : Acetone (12: 2.4)
Green	Pyridine: Glacial Acetic Acid:
	Acetonitrile : Water (3:3:3:1)

Typewriter Ribbon Ink

Ink from fabric-ribbon typewriter or dot matrix printer ribbons can be recognized by low-power microscopy as having a dull inked finish produced by impact. Ink from fabric ribbons or NCR impressions can usually be analyzed by TLC using a solvent of ethyl acetate, absolute ethanol, and water in ratios of 70:35:30 (ATF I), using pyridine as an extracting solvent.

Ink Jet Printer Ink

The ink jet printer is now the most common type of printer used with personal computers. You can analyze ink from ink jet printers using ATF I, which will often produce a chromatogram similar to that of ballpoint pen ink.

Test extracting solvents first on the document: Doherty[16] reported methanol and water 1:1 worked best. Some ink jets have a resin, which hardens with time and may interfere with extraction. If this seems to be the case, try pyridine as the extracting solvent.

TLC THEORY AND TECHNIQUE FOR INK ANALYSIS

We have presented TLC in detail due to its importance in ink analysis. The following is a brief overview of theory, terminology, and fine points of technique applicable to the above ink analysis procedures. Some of the subheadings below describe different aspects of the same step in the procedure; therefore, you should read the entire section prior to actually applying these steps.

Terminology[17]

ADSORBENT. A substance with which another substance undergoes *adsorption*; in TLC, this usually refers to the stationary phase. More commonly, the stationary phase or layer is termed the sorbent. In TLC, the stationary phase adsorbent is commonly alumina (Al_2O_3) or silica gel (silicic acid). The mobile phase (solvent system) migrates through the sorbent by capillary action. An inert binder attaches the TLC sorbent to the support plate. Silica gel is the adsorbent of choice for TLC of inks.

ADSORPTION. Intermolecular attraction and adhering of two substances. In TLC, the separation of the components in a mixture is caused by their repeated adsorption to and desorption from the stationary and mobile phases as the mobile phase undergoes movement by capillary action.

CAPILLARY ACTION (or Effect). The phenomenon by which a liquid (e.g., solvents of the solvent system) rises through a porous substance (e.g., thin layer stationary phase) as a result of a state in which intermolecular adhesion of the solvent molecules and the stationary phase particles is stronger than the forces between the solvent molecules themselves.

CHROMATOGRAPHIC POLARITY. Tendency of a substance to be held by the stationary phase. Chromatographic non-polarity is the tendency to migrate with the carrier solvent. Note that chromatographic polarity is distinguished from the ordinary use of the term "polarity" in chemistry, which means the presence of a dipole moment (molecular charge separation).

Distribution Coefficient (*Partition coefficient, partition ratio, distribution ratio*) (*k*). The ratio of the molar concentration of solute in the stationary phase to the mobile phase. The distribution coefficient is one factor that determines the migration rate of an analyte. The value of k is influenced by the temperature and concentration of the solute. When you analyze ink samples by TLC at different times or in different chambers, a difference in either of these two parameters can produce slightly different chromatograms for the same ink. There are other parameters that can also produce different chromatograms. Chamber saturation, plate activation/dryness, and solvent system preparation can also affect the results.[17]

ELUENT (*mobile phase/carrier solvent/solvent system/chromatographic solvent*). The eluent is a solvent or mixture of solvents comprising the mobile phase, the formula for which depends upon the type of analyte (ink). During chromatographic development, the mobile phase migrates by capillary action through the sorbent, dissolving and carrying with it the analyte. The mobile phase and analyte components undergo adsorption with the sorbent's active sites. The rate of migration of the mobile phase is a function of the strength of adsorption of the solvent with the sorbent. For any particular sorbent, the adsorption strength for a particular solvent is given by a eulotropic series. The solvent strength per unit area is expressed as the solvent strength parameter, ε°.

An eluent may also be a substance used in the manner described as "direct-elution" sample extraction, viz., a solvent, which passes through the paper medium to transfer the ink analyte to the plate surface.

SOLVENT SELECTIVITY. The characteristic of a solvent system, which produces, desired separation of components of an analyte. It is related to the distribution coefficient (above).[18]

Equipment Selection and Technique

PLATES. The term "high performance" designates plates with adsorptive layers of 200 μm or less. HPTLC plates also feature a smaller mean grain size–about 7 μm, as well as a closer grain distribution than conventional layers. These features of HPTLC plates provide superior resolution and shorter migration distance. Additionally, the optical properties of HPTLC plates are better than conventional layers, resulting in improved densitometric evaluation.[19] All of these features make HPTLC a choice technique for ink analysis.

Successful TLC analysis requires that the adsorbent and binder be inert to the extraction solvent, solvent system, and the analytes. Different support materials may produce different results due to interaction with the binder.[20] For ink analysis by TLC, all known government and private ink chemists use Merck® pre-coated silica gel, high-performance TLC plates. These plates provide excellent reproducibility and produce excellent resolution of dyes in inks.

The *active sites* on a silica gel plate are Si-OH groups–to which solvent and analyte adsorption occurs. In the TLC procedures, we list a preparative step of activating or heating the plate prior to use. This heating drives off moisture, which would otherwise mask many of the Si-OH sites. Do not exceed the recommended 100° C for 15 minutes, as this can cause a reduction of site activity with formation of inactive Si-O-Si linkages.[21]

Select TLC plates without fluorescent indicator. Such indicators are themselves fluorescent substances, e.g., zinc silicate and zinc sulfide, which are incorporated into the sorbent. When analyte components quench the indicator fluorescence, the components become visible under UV illumination as non-fluorescing bands. The presence of fluorescent indicators can mask UV fluorescence of ink components, eliminating one of the individualizing characteristics of an ink, visible in the TLC.[22]

Test whatever plates you plan to use and evaluate performance for ink analysis prior to casework. TLC Plate suppliers can supply technical advice for your applications.

Avoiding Plate Damage and Contamination

Do not use a plate whose sorbent layer has been scratched or marred. When you begin spotting ink extract, do not physically disturb the sorbent layer of the plate with the pipette or syringe needle as this can cause additional distortion of the chromatogram. Keep plates free of contamination from the time they are removed from packaging through use in developing chromatograms. In particular, see that spills, dripping, and spatter from reagents or samples cannot contaminate the plate surfaces during the process of preparing and spotting samples.

Solvent System

Use only reagent grade solvents for the solvent system (as well as sample extraction). Water should be distilled if possible. However, since questioned and known inks are compared on the same plate, the use of distilled water is not essential. Keep in mind when preparing the developing solvent that reagent "absolute" or 100% ethyl alcohol will undergo atmospheric saturation if exposed to air, diluting the ethanol. Additionally, some ethanol preparations are denatured. For this reason, some ink analysts use reagent grade ethyl alcohol. Actually, minor variations in solvent system formulation are not likely to significantly reduce their effectiveness so long as all compared samples are analyzed using the same preparation at the same time.

The ingredients of most ink TLC solvent systems have varying volatilities and will undergo different rates of evaporation once the solvent system is placed in the developing tank. Therefore, the proportions can change significantly over the period of a day. Touchstone recommended using an eluent only once if it is made up of more than one solvent.[23] With solvent systems designed for ink analysis, the authors have found that as many as three plates can be developed before changing the solvent system. However, if the tank has not been used recently, prepare a new developing solvent and let it equilibrate 15 minutes prior to developing the plate.

When you transfer the developing solvent to the tank, the solvent must produce a maximum level about 6 mm below the origin on the plate once the plate is placed into the tank.[24] If there is any question that the level of the carrier solvent may be too near the origin on the plate, then measure the actual level just prior to inserting the plate. To do this, set a narrow test plate into the tank, instantly remove it, and compare the adsorbed solvent level against the TLC plate with the spotted samples.

To complete preparation of the developing chamber, place a wick (made of a sheet of filtration, blotting, or chromatography paper) against the side after filling the tank with developing solvent. Next, close the tank and allow it to undergo atmospheric equilibration for at least 15 minutes, i.e., permit the atmosphere to become uniformly saturated with the solvent system.[25] Without saturation, the chromatogram can develop an "edge effect," i.e., a distortion of the solvent front along the vertical edge of the plate.

Ink Sample Sites

To preserve a file record of its unaltered appearance, photograph the original evidence with film photography, prior to ink sample removal. If photography is not possible, make a high-quality photocopy. Next, choose sites—in accordance with the following criteria:

- Minimizing damage to the document or the readability of its contents.
- Maximizing ink mass removed per linear measure.
- Avoiding contamination of the ink sample.

Record these sites on a photocopy of the questioned document. Pre-label corresponding temporary sample containers to receive samples from those sites. Mark temporary containers, e.g., 5 gr. vials, with an indelible pen to indicate the number of the sample site.

Ink Sample Removal

After you finish labeling all containers and mapping sampling sites, prepare ink samples by physically removing approximately 1 mm O.D. ink-coated paper plugs (called microdots or microplugs) from the questioned document at the chosen sample sites. You can use an ink sampling punch (a blunt No. 16–20 gauge hypodermic needle) with sharpened and flattened circular edge, or a device specifically designed for ink plug removal such as the *Micro-Punch*™ by *Premier Scientific.*[26]

If there is any printing or writing on the document's side opposite the sampling sites, examine the document with fiber optic backlighting to avoid choosing sites that correspond to this potential contamination. If the paper is two-ply, an additional remedy to avoid contamination is to cut and remove microplugs from the top layer of the document while taking care not to acquire opposite-side ink in the sample.

Match the sample site with the labeled temporary container and, once spotting is finished, match the sample with the correct origin position on the TLC plate.

Paper Controls

In addition to ink samples on each TLC plate, include a paper control (a plug of a blank portion of paper near the ink sampling sites) for each ink sample that you remove from a different paper surface. In the developed chromatogram, note whether the paper control contributed any bands in the ink chromatogram. If so, you know that the substances represented by these bands are not part of the ink formulations.

Avoiding Contamination

If the same punch is used to remove different ink samples (especially samples to be compared against each other), it is important that no trace of contaminate from one sample remain in the punch. The authors have found that dry ink samples removed from paper will not generally cross-contaminate from one sample to another. However, if necessary, clean the punch with air or solvent between samplings and dry thoroughly prior to subsequent use.

Extraction

Once you remove samples and place them into temporary sample containers, you will need to extract the ink samples from the paper plugs, to spot the ink onto the TLC plates.

Extraction of ink from paper plugs involves placing equal numbers of plugs into vials with extraction solvent. Quality control requires that all compared samples be extracted using the same conditions. The numbers of plugs, type and volume of solvent, time in solvent, temperature, and stirring or agitation must be the same. (An alternative extraction procedure called "Direct Elution" will be discussed later.)

Spotting Preparation

To spot the samples, you will need a micropipette. Harris suggests using a *Drummond Digital Microdispenser*, which permits 0.01 microliter increments up to 10-microliter total volume.[27] The authors use a 10 microliter pipette.

Spot Position and Alignment

Spot samples well above the level the solvent will reach in the developing chamber and sufficiently spaced apart that they will not laterally elute into one another during chromatographic development. All spots should be equidistant from the bottom of the plate so that the solvent reaches them all at the same time as the chromatogram begins development.

The minimum distance required between spots will depend to some extent upon how small you can make the spots. Generally, about 1 cm should separate all spots.

Regarding vertical placement, misalignment of spots may cause R_f variations between equivalent bands of identical samples. Because of the high visibility of inks, the alignment of their origin spots will be conspicuous as soon as you produce each spot. If you misalign any spot, you should disregard the chromatogram for that spot. You can then spot the sample at a different location along the line of the origin or discard the plate altogether. This can be a critical problem if the ink sample is in short supply, which is often the case in forensic ink analysis.

There are a number of tools available to properly align spots. TLC overlay spotting templates feature a raised section to fit over the TLC plate. The template has an alignment edge for correctly positioning the TLC plate and has measured notches along the sample application points for guiding the pipette to the surface. Lewis suggests spotting exactly 19 mm from the plate base, with solvent level at 13 mm.[28]

Approximately Equal and Optimum Sample Mass

Spot approximately equal masses of sample at each origin position. If you spot samples of widely differing masses of ink, the resulting chromatograms may be difficult to interpret. Faint bands visible in the sample of higher mass may be undetectable in the in the chromatogram which develops from the sample of lesser mass. Approximately equal masses of ink per unit volume are prepared by using equal numbers of ink plugs for each sample. Each plug should have the same number of ink layers, extracted in the same solvent under the same conditions for the same length of time. As a rough measure, you can backlight the vials prior to spotting and visually compare the relative optical density of each. However, slight differences in ink concentrations will not affect the developed TLC.

After extraction, fill the micropipette with the extract and completely apply a pre-determined volume of each dissolved ink to the plate at the origin. Spot intermittently at the origin for each sample to keep the spot small. The combination of about 10 plugs of ink from the written line placed into 1–2 drops of solvent will normally produce the optimum ink mass. The optimum mass range for the development of a good chromatogram is small enough to produce good separation. It also provides sufficient mass of all separated components to be detectible.

If you spot too much sample, "overloading" occurs. This is a condition where migration of the ink components is impaired, potentially masking components with close R_f values. This is seen when the ink chromatogram forms streaks in lanes where distinct bands should be. In extreme cases of overloading, the migrating solvent will take the path of least resistance and go around the origin spot. You can determine this optimum mass range through practice.[29] The techniques described here will not lead to overloaded spots.

Once you begin spotting, use the entire volume of ink for each sample. In other words, do not base the application of ink sample upon the number of drops that touch and adsorb at the origin. The latter method can cause subtle measurement errors.[30] The object of this whole process is to apply approximately equal amounts of all inks being compared.

Solvent Release

Keep the spots small. If you allow too much extraction solvent to be applied to the TLC plate at once, the dilute solution of ink will undergo radial chromatographic development and form a ring of ink at the origin. A defective spot can result in a defective chromatogram and produce double bands for the same components. The degree of spreading at the origin is related to the R_f of the ink components as they undergo radial chromatographic development in the extraction solvent (not the developing solvent). A low R_f means less spreading of the origin spot.[31]

To Keep the Spot Small Use These Three Techniques:

- Control the flow to the TLC plate by lifting the micropipette off the plate as soon as the spot is made and then spot again, as necessary. This keeps too much ink extract from being dispensed each time the pipette comes into contact with the plate. Pyridine, the commonly used extraction solvent for ballpoint inks, spreads rapidly on a TLC plate surface.
- Allow the spot to air dry—about 10 seconds or until the solvent appears to have evaporated—between each application.
- Apply the pipette or syringe needle to precisely the same pinpoint position on the plate with each application.

Spot Drying Prior to TLC Development

As soon as you have finished spotting, allow spots to air dry for about 20–30 minutes or heat at about 80° C for 10 minutes.

Plate Placement

When the tank and plate are ready, carefully place the plate into the tank so that the base of the plate is level with the bottom of the tank. Let the top of the plate lean against the side of the tank so that no part of the tank or wick touches the sides or developing surface of the plate. If you have pre-tested the developing solvent level to insure that it lies below the origin spots, then the solvent level should be safely below the spots.

Once the plate is placed into the tank, quickly close the tank to minimize loss of atmospheric saturation. Cover the tank with a glass plate, preferably with a grease-coating seal. During development, do not bump or otherwise move the tank. Any physical disturbance of the tank can potentially propel the developing solvent from the reservoir onto or above the origin spots, disrupting the process of chromatographic development.

As soon as the chromatogram has undergone sufficient development (about 15 minutes), remove the plate from the tank or developing chamber. Lightly mark the solvent front with a pencil on the plate at the time of removal for future reference in determining the R_f values.

Reading TLC Plates

R_f Measurements

R_f ("R-F"), which stands for *Retention Factor*, is the distance from the origin to the band in the developed chromatogram divided by the distance from the origin to the solvent front. In thin layer chromatography, R_f is an important identifying characteristic of a band in a TLC.

Make measurements for R_f from the center of the origin to the center of the band in the developed chromatogram. Measure the migration of the solvent from the center of the origin to the solvent front location at the time the plate was removed, in the same lane as the compared band.[32]

Since they are ratios of distance, R_f values have no units. R_f values are stated from 0, for a non-migrating substance to 0.999, for a band that has essentially migrated to the solvent front.[33]

When bands of two samples are compared, calculate and compare the R_f values–or visually estimate the R_f of the bands and note whether all have equal or different R_f values. You can also determine R_f values using commercially available R_f readers. In practice, R_f values can usually be calculated to one, possibly two significant figures. R_f values may vary with the variable parameters of the TLC procedure and development conditions. Therefore, all parameters should be the same, if you are comparing R_f values of dye bands in different samples.

R_f values, alone, represent only a presumptive identifier of the substance contained in the TLC band; however, for purposes of ink analysis, you already know the general category of the analyte (dye band) at the outset. By knowing the source of the analyte as a written ink line or pen, you have reasonably limited the set of possible substances represented by the TLC bands, prior to chemical analysis. In addition, common dye components and their R_f values are known, as well as their characteristic colors. Thus, frequently, an ink component's R_f, along with its color, can identify it as a particular chemical compound with a considerable degree of confidence.

If you compare a band against a known standard, you may use the relative retention value, R_x, as a means of comparison. R_x is the ratio of the distance the questioned band migrates to the distance the known standard migrates. If the questioned analyte migrates further than the known standard, R_x will be greater than one.[34]

Video Spectral and Color Analysis of Ink Chromatograms

Video spectral and UV fluorescence/absorbance comparison of ink lines is covered in Chapter 4, as is visual color assessment. The same principles apply to examination and comparison of ink component bands in thin layer chromatograms.[35]

Technical Notes/Worksheet

An ink analysis worksheet is necessary to record your results, comments, and conclusions. These notes are used to prepare a formal report of your findings. The information contained in your formal report should be entirely consistent with that contained in your worksheet. The worksheet is also essential for technical review of your work should you be called upon to testify at a later date. Keep in mind that opposing counsel may ask to review your worksheet at the time of your testimony and you must be prepared to explain any entries you make.

The information that you choose to record and the printed format of your worksheet is dictated by the equipment that you have available for ink analysis and by your laboratory's written protocol. As discussed throughout this book, there are published protocols for ink analysis; thus, your written protocol and worksheet format should be consistent with those which have been peer reviewed or standardized and published. Possible formats for an ink analysis and TLC worksheet are provided in Figures 5.6 and 5.7.

Ink Analysis Worksheet

Date Documents Were Received: _____   How Received: _____   Date of Examination: _____

Sample No.	Description of Entry	No. Of Microplugs	Color of Ink	Type of Ink	Solvent	Color of Ink in Solvent	IR LUM	IR REFL.	UV	Type of Paper	Other Observations
1	Initials "JD" next to numerical entry "$500,000"	10	black	BP	Pyridine	Blue-green	Pos	Opaque	neg	white bond	signature was water stained
2											
3											
4											
5											
6											
7											
8											
9											
10											
11											
12											
13											
14											
15											

Notes:

Figure 5.6. Ink analysis worksheet.

TLC Worksheet

Merck HPTLC _____ **minutes in Solvent System I**
Merck HPTLC _____ **minutes in Solvent System II**
Other _____ **minutes in Solvent System** _____

Relative Aging:

Ten plugs of samples 1,2, and 3 extracted ½, 1 ½, and 3 minutes with 20 ul of 1-butanol and 4 ul aliquots spotted. After drying, remaining ink extracted with 10 ul of benzyl alcohol for 5 minutes. – 4 ul spotted.

Accelerated Aging:

Ten plugs of samples 1, 2, and 3 heated 30 minutes at 100 degrees C. After cooling, relative aging described above was performed.

Tags Detected   A and B in sample 2

Matching Inks: Samples 1 and 3 match and also match a Bic black BP ink standard. Sample No. 2 matches a Formulab black BP ink standard.

Results of Relative Aging:

Samples 1 and 3 have the same relative age. Heated samples of 1 and 3 produced substantially different percent and rates of extractions, compared to the unheated samples.

Conclusion:

Samples 1 and 3 were written at the same time, some time within the last 3 years of this date. These inks could not have been written in 1989 (the date of the document), over 10 years. Sample no. 2 appears to be totally dry and therefore could have been written in 1989.

Other Notes:

Figure 5.7. TLC worksheet.

Alternative TLC Devices and Methods

AUTOMATIC SPOTTERS. If you are working with a large number of ink samples, you can use an automatic spotter to save time, but be sure to test such a device prior to actual casework. It is unlikely that it was designed specifically for ink analysis.

Sample Extraction/Spotting Option II: Direct-Elution

An alternative method of ink extraction and spotting commonly called "direct-elution" was described by Kurantz.[36] To use this method, place a single microplug, ink-down at the origin on the TLC plate. Fill the pipette or syringe with a predetermined volume of pure extracting solvent and then carefully touch it to the top (un-inked) side of the microplug. Slowly release the solvent. The solvent flows through the microplug and elutes the ink onto the thin layer plate, forming the origin spot. If the first extraction solvent does not fully transfer the ink to the plate, you can use a second solvent, so long as you use the same volume of each extracting solvent for all compared samples. Kurantz favors using a mixture of n-butanol, isopropanol, and water (2:1:1 by volume) first, followed by pyridine (if necessary).

This technique has the advantage that it is quicker than pre-extraction and can often permit spotting of a suitable amount of ink from a single microplug to produce a definitive chromatogram. The efficient use of solvent and the option of using multiple extraction solvents maximize the ink extraction and the ink concentration in the origin spot. This technique also permits use of a non-disposable microsyringe, which will not cause sample cross-contamination since only pure extraction solvent is introduced into the syringe. There are four potential problems associated with direct-elution:

- It does not permit the density adjustment one can perform with pre-extraction.
- It requires considerable care and dexterity to perform. A single microplug when manipulated in this manner can be lost to the slightest air draft. Even vent hood air drafts can present a problem—and you will probably need to use a vent hood whenever you work with pyridine, even in minute quantities.
- The origin spot must be microscopically examined after spotting to be certain that no paper fragment remains at the origin. Such a fragment can cause development of a defective chromatogram.
- Some dye components may not completely extract. This can cause errors in quantitative densitometer measurements.

Multiple Development

If one solvent system does not produce clearly separated dyes in the ink, the ink samples can be compared with a second solvent system, provided there is sufficient sample to permit such a retest.

Research by Resua et al. on textile dyes (which applies to ink dyes as well) indicates that multiple solvent system results are more significant if they produce different R_f values.[37] These are termed "non-correlated systems." As in other testing procedures, multiple development may not be an option if ink samples are limited in amount.

Two-Dimensional TLC

An option that can yield higher separation efficiency is two-dimensional TLC. The procedure for 2-D TLC is as follows:
- Deposit only one spot on a TLC plate. To locate the proper site for your origin spot, measure in from the edge of the plate the same distance that you measure up from the bottom edge of the plate. For example, if you use the standard of 19 mm from the bottom of the plate, measure the same lateral distance from the left or right side of the plate to place the spot. Develop the chromatogram in the normal fashion.
- Remove the plate from the chamber.
- Dry and place into the chamber again; this time rotated 90 degrees from the original orientation, with the bands of the original chromatogram now forming origin spots for a second chromatographic development.
- In the second development, use a different solvent system than used the first time.

The goal is to choose a second solvent system that more efficiently separates components contained in bands or in incompletely resolved bands of the first chromatographic separation.

The main limitation of 2-D TLC is that it is not a parallel system, i.e., you can only run one sample per plate.

Preadsorbent and Dual Adsorbent Plates

These alternative plates are not commonly used in ink analysis; however, they might be used in future research.

Preadsorbent TLC plates are manufactured with a "preadsorbent" area, which allows the eluting solvent to dissolve the analyte and produce a tighter band before it reaches the "main" separation area. The greater concentration of the band can result in higher resolution in the developed chromatogram. If you wish to use this feature, consult the plate manufacturer for current product applications.[38]

Dual adsorbent plates have one type adsorbent along the edge for the first development–and a second type of adsorbent in the remaining area of the plate. In this fashion, a second chromatogram is developed using yet another parameter, with the objective of producing additional separations.[39]

Comparison of Thin Layer Chromatography with Other Techniques

Compared to other ink analysis techniques, TLC offers the following advantages:

- SENSITIVITY AND DISCRIMINATION. TLC is an especially sensitive technique for ink analysis, in part because of the intense color of dye components. With TLC, you can characterize an ink sample of as little as 0.10 microgram and compare it with other ink samples. With the well-researched solvent systems available today, most ink formulations are readily distinguishable by TLC.
- ECONOMY. The equipment necessary for TLC is extraordinarily inexpensive as analytical techniques go. Fixed equipment consists of a vent hood (which most laboratories already have in place) and a suitable developing tank. Consumable items incur little expense mainly because solvent use is minimal. Reagents, plates, sampling and spotting equipment necessary for a forensic laboratory's typical yearly caseload are generally a few hundred dollars. The only additional expenses involve equipment for evaluation of TLC plates, including video spectral units (used by most forensic document labs) and TLC scanners (scanning densitometers).
- SPEED. A TLC plate can be developed in less than 20 minutes. For larger numbers of samples, the process of sample spotting may be the most time-consuming step, unless automated equipment is used for the spotting. While TLC is a fast technique, ink analysis may require time-consuming and tedious sample preparation, which is required of any semi-destructive technique.
- SMALL SAMPLE REQUIREMENT. A few microplugs are usually sufficient for TLC analysis. You can perform TLC using the Direct-Elution technique, with a single microplug, ca. 1.0 mm O.D.
- QUICK CHANGE OF VARIABLE PARAMETERS. You can prepare different plates or solvent systems in minutes.

DENSITOMETRY

Theory and Instrumentation

A scanning TLC densitometer measures optical density or fluorescence of each band over the length of a chromatogram. On the plotter chart, optical density is represented on the vertical axis, with the horizontal axis of the spectrum representing distance from the origin. The measurement units are linear. Peak integration of optical density reveals sample mass, producing a quantitative measure of the concentration of dyes in the TLC bands.

There are currently two types of densitometers, generally termed: classical (spectrometer) and video.[40] The classical densitometer can be set for a specific detection wavelength and light beam area. This instrument measures the transmitted or reflected light with a photo-electric detector.

By contrast, the video densitometer generates an electronic image of the plate, and converts the intensities of image pixels into optical density measurements.

The first section of this chapter describes specific procedures for ink thin layer densitometry. The densitometer measures optical density of the bands against the blank sorbent of the TLC plate. A classical double-beam scanning densitometer produces a reference signal of the sorbent in a lane adjacent to that of the sampled chromatogram to account for any sorbent non-uniformity. When using a double-beam densitometer, you must provide sufficient blank sorbent lanes adjacent to each lane to accommodate this reference beam.

Depending on design of the particular instrument, densitometers can be operated in transmission or reflectance mode, or both simultaneously. In transmission, absorbance measurements follow Beer's Law (measurements are linear).

$$A = \varepsilon bC$$
Beer's Law
A = absorbance ε = molar absorptivity
b = path length C = concentration

In densitometry of thin layer chromatograms, slight deviations from Beer's Law are due to scatter of illumination caused by the turbidity of the sorbent. This is explained more fully by a generalization of Beer's

Law, the Kubelka Munk theory. A simplified but adequate form of Kubelka Munk,[41] which describes transmittance and reflectance of a turbid sheet, is given by the following formula:

$$\text{Transmittance } A_T \cong e^{-\gamma x}$$

$$\text{Reflectance } A_R \cong \frac{K-\gamma}{K+\gamma}$$

$$\text{Where } \gamma = \sqrt{(2S+K)K}$$

Kubela Munk formula for transmittance and reflectance on a TLC plate

S = Scattering power of the medium

K = coefficient of absorption of the sheet material

X = thickness   γ = transmittance of a very thin layer

At low concentrations (those normally examined in TLC densitometry), the analyte increases the absorption within its absorbing region of the spectrum and scatter has a negligible effect.

Sources of Error from Analytical Data

The purpose of densitometric measurements of ink thin layer chromatograms is to determine ink dye component concentration with the greatest possible reliability.[42] A "reliable" measurement is one which is both accurate and precise, and one that reveals exactly the true value.

Both "wet" chemistry, such as TLC, and chemical instrumental analysis, such as densitometry, have their own accuracy and precision. Accuracy is the measure of how close the measured value is to the true value–regardless of the spread of the measured value. Inaccuracy is caused by systematic errors. Precision, by contrast, is the closeness of independent tests to a single value–regardless of whether they are close to the true value. Imprecision is caused by random errors.

Some texts speak of a "gross error." This is a serious instrument malfunction or procedural error, which, if recognized, requires disregarding results and retesting.[43]

Error Correction

Systematic instrument errors will usually be revealed with repeated measurements as a bias–an error of equal magnitude and direction. These errors are detected and corrected through testing with calibration standards, prior to casework.

Correction of systematic human errors requires that the operator be skilled and capable of properly operating the instrument, and capable of performing the wet chemical procedures.

Random errors of combined TLC and densitometry can be assessed by statistical analysis of measurement data. Most of the random errors detected from multiple tests involving separate sample removal, extraction, spotting, and, where relevant, TLC development, arise from the analyst's technique—not the instrumental measurements. Touchstone and Sherma note that this is a general principle in TLC densitometry.[44] Random instrument errors are relatively small.

Table 5.2
COMPONENTS OF RELIABILITY

Requirement	Type Error	Method of Error Correction
Accuracy	Systematic	Human Practice and skill
		Instrument Calibration
Precision	Random	Statistical Analysis

Precision Assessment through Statistical Analysis of Measurements

To achieve maximum precision of combined TLC and densitometric measurements, perform duplicate or triplicate analyses of ink samples (as sample quantity permits), then use statistical analysis to determine the mean and spread of the densitometric data. The following is a brief summary of the steps used in statistical evaluation of densitometric data from thin layer chromatography.

Determine the Mean Concentration for Each Sample

$$\bar{x} = \frac{(\Sigma x)}{n}$$

Formula for Mean

Where n = number of measurements, x = general piece of data
for the set of measurements

Determine Standard Deviation (SD)

$$SD = \sqrt{\frac{\Sigma(x - \bar{x})^2}{n - 1}}$$

Formula for Standard Deviation

Determine Confidence Intervals

The standard deviation provides a measure of the precision for measurements on a single sample spot or band and is expressed in the same units as that of the original measurements. Standard deviation permits calculation of confidence intervals for the individual measurements.

Chebyshev's theorem states that with any distribution, a minimum of 75% of the values will fall within +/- 2 standard deviations of the mean; 89% within 3 standard deviations. With enough measurements, random errors of measurement will be expected to produce a normal (bell) curve. If this is the case, then 68% of the measurements will fall within 1 standard deviation, 95% within 2 standard deviations, and about 99% within 3 standard deviations. This means, for instance, that there is a 95% probability that the "true" value is within 2 standard deviations of the mean, assuming neither the instrument nor human factors contribute systematic error.

Statistical Determination of Ink Age Differences

Ink dating by TLC and densitometry is taken up in Chapter 8. In that chapter you will find a discussion of statistical analysis of data as it relates to ink age differences.

Relative Standard Deviation

While you can use the standard deviation as a measure of spread of the values of a set of measurements for one data set, the relative standard deviation (also called Coefficient of Variation) is a relative measure of spread for data sets with different units or magnitudes, expressed as a percentage relative uncertainty.

$$100 \text{ X } \frac{\text{SD}}{\bar{\text{x}}}$$

Formula for Relative Standard Deviation

Measurement Precision Variations of Different Instrument Parameters

When using a spectrometer densitometer, you may need to compare relative precision of beam slit measurements. The simplest method is to perform transmittance or reflectance measurements on undeveloped spots produced with increasing numbers of microplugs,

e.g., 10–25, in 5-plug increments. Compare relative standard deviations in each mode, for plugs of each mass.[45] Note that you are not
required to perform this procedure before each analysis.

Table 5.3
GENERALIZED CHART FOR STATISTICAL COMPARISON
OF INSTRUMENT PARAMETERS

Number of Microplugs	Peak Area	Statistical
		SD
		RSD

If one beam slit shows a lower relative standard deviation, it is superior. If the relative standard deviation of each is approximately the
same, they can be associated with equal precision.

Tests of Multiple Microplugs to Demonstrate Equal Mass Per Microplug and to Determine Working Range

Graphic linearity (within some region of the graph) of a scatter plot
of data points of the number of ink microplugs plotted against average
area establishes the following:
- Adherence to Beer's Law (approximate).
- Equal measure of ink in microplugs (but never exactly equal).
- Number of microplugs to test.

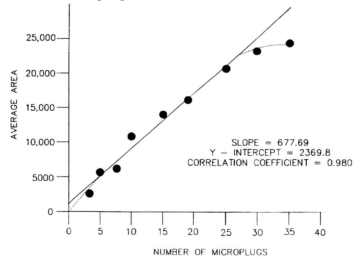

Figure 5.8. Peak area for ink or dye vs. number of microplugs.[46]

If an increasing number of microplugs graph as a straight line (for some region of the graph) vs. densitometric measurement of mass, then you know that the individual microplugs have approximately equal masses of ink and that, in this region, Beer's Law is being roughly followed. Because densitometry involves a sample on a turbid medium, Beer's Law is only followed for samples of relatively low mass. There will be a range of known mass (numbers of microplugs) for which this graph is linear. This should be the "working range" of microplug samples. Above the "working range" the graph is no longer linear (see Figure 5.8).

For one test of ballpoint ink entries, Brunelle and Lee experimentally determined the known mass for a working range for densitometry, as well as the statistically significant linearity deviations.[47] The procedure is as follows:

- Plot average area of optical density peaks for samples against increasing numbers of microplugs.
- A useful number of microplugs is 5–20, in 5-plug increments, dissolved in 20 µl of pyridine.
- Evaluate precision of measurements by calculating standard deviation and compare relative standard deviation for each set of scans for each number of plugs.
- Find the "fitted line" for the graph (the line should pass through the origin, where the X and Y axes meet).

Fitted Line Determination

The "fitted line" can be determined several ways, including calculation of the correlation coefficient (CV). The formula for CV for variables x and y, is:

$$r = \frac{1}{n-1} \sum \left(\frac{x - \bar{x}}{s_x} \right) \left(\frac{y - \bar{y}}{s_y} \right)$$

Correlation Coefficient (r) for variables S_x and S_y

The correlation coefficient of the graph is a measurement from -1 to +1. The sign indicates the slope of the line. The slope, in turn, indicates the correlation (+ = up, i.e., positive correlation between the variables being compared). How close the points are to the line is indicated by the absolute value of the correlation coefficient, where 1 = values lying exactly along the line).

Statistical methods are available to determine effect of marked deviations (e.g., outliers) on the fit of the line.

Applied to densitometry measurements of increasing numbers of microplugs, a positive slope with a correlation coefficient near 1 is evidence of a positive adherence to Beer's Law for the measurements. The working range for numbers of microplugs will be the region of the graph where these requirements are most closely met. If the graph levels off, then absorbance measurements no longer differentiate between different masses of sample. Brunelle and Lee found an average relative standard deviation of 4.0% (judged as insignificant) in one test of ballpoint inks.[48]

You can also compare FTIR spectra using correlation coefficients. This will be discussed in the section on Fourier transform infrared spectrometry in Chapter 6.

Standard Error and Significant Digits

Standard Error (SE)—also known as Standard Deviation of the Mean is a statistical tool that allows you to accurately express measurements. The first non-zero digit in the SE is the last significant digit for the mean value.

$$SE = \frac{SD}{\sqrt{n}}$$

Formula for SE

We have provided only a brief summary of statistics applied to densitometry in thin layer chromatography. For a more in-depth treatment, many texts, professional publications, and resources on the World Wide Web are available.

Resources for Statistical Analysis of Chemical Data

- *Practice for Conducting an Interlaboratory Study to Determine the Precision of a Test Method*, ASTM Designation E 691.
- *Standard Terminology for Relating to Quality and Statistics*, ASTM Designation E 456–96.
- *Standard Practice for Use of Statistics in the Evaluation of Spectrometric*

Data, ASTM Designation E 876–89.
- *Statistical Manual of the Association of Official Analytical Chemists*, W. J. Youden and E. H. Steiner, 1975.

Resources on Thin Layer Chromatography

- *Handbook of Thin-Layer Chromatography*, Joseph Sherma and Bernard Fried, Marcel Dekker, Inc., Publisher, 1996.
- *Densitometry in Thin Layer Chromatography*, Joseph Touchstone, Joseph Sherma, John Wiley & Sons, 1979.
- *The Practice of Thin Layer Chromatography*, Joseph C. Touchstone, John Wiley & Sons, 1992.
- *Thin-Layer Chromatography: Techniques and Application*, Bernard Fried and Joseph Sherma.
- *Standard Guide for Test Methods for Forensic Writing Ink Identifications. Annual Book of ASTM Standards*, 14.02: Section 14, 903, 1996.

REFERENCES

1. Brunelle, R. L. & Pro, M. J.: A Systematic approach to ink identification. *JAOAC*, 55: 823, 1972.
2. Brunelle, R. & Reed, R.: *Forensic Examination of Ink and Paper.* Springfield, IL, Charles C Thomas, 1984.
3. Brunelle, R. L. & Lee, H.: Determining the relative age of ballpoint ink using a single solvent extraction mass independent approach. *JFS*, 34: 1166, 1989.
4. Lyter, A. L.: Examination of ball pen ink by high pressure liquid chromatography. *JFS*, 1: 339, 1984.
5. Tibbet, I. R., Chem, C., Fitzgerald, M. & Olson, L.: The use of HPLC with multiwavelength detection for the differentiation of non ball pen inks. *JFS*, 37: 1149, 1992.
6. Liu, H., Zhu, T., Zhang, Y., Qi, S., Huang, A. & Sun, Y.: Determination of synthetic colorant food additives by capillary zone electrophoresis. *J. Chromatography*, 718: 448, 1995.
7. Fanali, S. & Schudel, S.: Some separation of black and red water-soluble fiber tip pen inks by capillary zone electrophoresis and thin-layer chromatography. *JFS*, 36: 1192, 1991.
8. Stewart, L.: Ballpoint ink age determination by volatile component comparison—a preliminary study. *JFS*, 30: 405, 1985.
9. Aginsky, V.: Dating and characterizing writing, stamp pad and jet printer inks by gas chromatography/mass spectrometry. *Int. J. Forensic Document Examiners*, 2: 103, 1996.
10. Xu, X., deKoeijer, J. A., deMoel, J. J. M. & Logtenberg, H.: Ink analysis for

forensic science applications by micellar electrokinetic capillary chromatography with photo diode array detection. *Int. J. Forensic Document Examiners*, 3: 240, 1997.

11. Tebbett, I. R.: Chromatographic analysis of inks for forensic science applications. *For. Sci.Review*, 3: 71, 1991.

12. Standard guide for test methods for forensic writing ink identifications. *Annual Book of ASTM Standards*, 14.02: Section 14, 903, 1996.

13. Standard guide for test methods for forensic writing ink comparisons. *Annual Book of ASTM Standards*, 13.01: ASTM designation: E1422–91. 1992.

14. Aginsky, V. N.: *JFS* 38/5: P.1131–1133, September, 1993.

15. Jasuja, O. P. & Sharma, R.: Printing Inks. *Int. J. Forensic Document Examiners*, 3/4: 356–359, December, 1997.

16. Doherty, P.: Classification of ink jet printers and inks. *Journal of ASQDE*, 12/98; pp. 88–96.

17. Touchstone, J. C.: *The Practice of Thin Layer Chromatography*. John Wiley & Sons, 1992.

18. Ibid.

19. CAMAG Scientific, 2000 Catalog.

20. Lewis, J.: Thin-layer chromatography of writing inks–Quality control considerations. *JFS*, 41/5: 874–877, 1996.

21. Peters, D. G., Hayes, J. M. & Heifje, G. M.: *Chemical Separations and Measurements*. p. 555, W. B. Saunders, 1974.

22. Skoog, D. A.: *Principles of Instrumental Analysis*. p. 665, Saunders College Publishing, 1971.

23. See 17 above.

24. See 20 above.

25. Ibid.

26. Premier Scientific P. O. Box 42057 Ottawa, Ontario, Canada K1K 4L8.

27. Harris, J.: Developments in the analysis of writing inks on questioned documents. *JFS* 37/2:612–619, March, 1992.

28. See 20 above.

29. See 17 above.

30. Ibid.

31. Sherma, J.: *Practice and Applications of Thin Layer Chromatography on Whatman High Performance Silica Plates*. TLC Technical Series, Vol 2, p. 4.

32. See 17 above.

33. Ibid.

34. Ibid.

35. *Densitometric Chromatogram Evaluation*, CAMAG Scientific, http://www.camag.ch/katauswe.htm.

36. Kuranz, R. L.: Technique for transferring ink from a written line to a thin-layer chromatographic sheet. *JFS*, 31/2: 665–657, April, 1986.

37. Resua, R., De Forest, P. R. & Harris, H.: The evaluation and selection of uncorrelated paired solvent systems for use in the comparison of textile dyes by TLC. *JFS*, 26/3: 515–534, July 1981.

38. Alltech Chromatography Catalog 300, p.426.

39. Ibid.

40. See 35 above.

41. Touchstone, J. & Sherma, J.: *Densitometry in Thin Layer Chromatography.* New York: John Wiley & Sons, 1979, p. 44.

42. Cantu, A. A.: A sketch of analytical methods for document dating part II: Determining age dependent analytical profiles. *IJFDE*, Vol. 2, No. 3, July/Sept. 1996, p. 194.

43. Miller, J. C. & Miller, J. N.: *Statistics for Analytical Chemistry*, 1988, p. 17.

44. Touchstone, J. & Sherma, J.: *Densitometry in Thin Layer Chromatography.* New York: John Wiley & Sons, 1979, p. 109.

45. Brunelle, R. L. & Lee, H.: Determining the relative age of ballpoint ink using a single-solvent extraction, mass-independent approach. *JFS 35*(5); Sept., 1989, pp. 1166–1182.

46. Ibid (p. 1172).

47. Ibid.

48. Ibid.

Chapter 6

INSTRUMENTAL ANALYSIS OF INKS

Thin layer chromatography, video spectral analysis TLC densitometry, and microscopy will usually permit satisfactory comparison of writing inks; however, you may encounter inks that require additional instrumental techniques that offer different discrimination. These techniques include analysis by UV-VIS-NIR microspectrophotometry, Fourier transform infrared spectroscopy, Raman spectroscopy, liquid chromatography, capillary electrophoresis and mass spectrometry.

SPECTROSCOPY

Theory

Spectroscopy is a technique for resolving electromagnetic radiation into its component wavelengths and measuring the radiation as it interacts with matter. Spectroscopic analyses produce charts of absorption, transmittance, or emission measured against wavelength, wavenumber, or, in Raman spectroscopy—wavenumber shift.

Spectroscopic analysis of inks on documents can be non-destructive or semi-destructive. Semi-destructive techniques require removal of one ink-coated paper fiber or application of a small amount of colloidal metal to the sample site.

A rapid and accurate means of sampling color, storing, and comparing colors is through use of visible light microspectrophotometry. Using computer software, this technique converts reflectance data into color space coordinates. The same instrument can produce a reflectance spectrum. Both are objective, linear representations of color.

Color Space and Visible Spectrophotometry

L. Keith Kerr analyzed ballpoint inks with color space microspectrophotometry using multivariant statistical analysis of chromaticity data. He reported a 43% increase in discrimination over IR video spectral examination and an 8.0% improvement over spectrophotometry alone (visible range).[1] This technique places the object's color at a "chromaticity point" defined by the complementary chromaticity coordinates within the color space diagram.

An elliptical "error region" can be constructed around a statistical mean chromaticity point so that mean values for compared samples which fall within the ellipse an be considered "matches." Those outside the ellipse are considered differentiated. The greatest accuracy is achieved when the ellipse is small.

In Kerr's study, reflectance spectra were recorded from 10 different areas within the ink stroke to generate data for creation of the ellipse. He achieved excellent reproducibility of complementary chromaticity points for each spot. This method represents one of several non-destructive means of analysis.

Ultraviolet-Visible-Near Infrared (UV-VIS-NIR) Microspectrophotometry and Microspectrofluorimetry

Ulrich Seipp at Kriminaltechisches Institut, Wiesbaden, Germany used UV-VIS-NIR microspectrophotometry and microspectrofluorimetry to compare ballpoint pen inks, pure ballpoint ink dyes, and color copier toner particles.[2]

This analysis is performed directly on the document, thus reflectance microspectrophotometry is non-destructive. In transmitted mode, destruction is negligible, requiring a single paper fiber with ink for examination. The fiber is embedded in glycerine, on a quartz microscope slide with a glass cover-slip.

Seipp reported ink discrimination with both reflected and transmitted microspectrophotometry modes; however, he encountered a few difficulties in reflectance mode:

1. Differences in microscopic surface characteristics ("inhomogenieties") required multiple sampling to achieve reproducibility.
2. When glass objectives were used, UV registration was limited to no less than 380 nm.

3. Use of UV-transmitting fiber optics, useful for incident sample irradiation, precluded use of shortwave UV.

Microspectrophotometry could not discriminate ballpoint inks as effectively as TLC or HPLC. The reason is that spectra obtained by microspectrophotometry are based upon analysis of whole ink, while chromatographic techniques separate the many ink components. TLC separation allows analysis of the pure components by color, R_f and video spectral responses.

Limitations of microspectrophotometry in the ultraviolet are noteworthy since the UV region contributes significantly to differentiation of several ballpoint inks that were not distinguishable in other spectral regions.

Figure 6.1 shows clearly distinguishable UV/visible range transmission spectra of blue ballpoint inks. Microspectrophotometric analysis of the substance is made on a quartz slide.

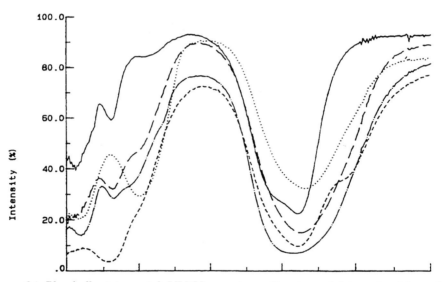

Figure 6.1. Blue ballpoint pen ink UV/Vis spectrum. Courtesy of *International Journal of Forensic Document Examiners.*

UV-VIS-NIR Reflectance Microspectrophotometry

Josey et al. compared two spectrometers, the Foster & Freeman VSC2000 microspectrometer and the Ziess MPM microspectrophotometer for ink differentiation.[3] Foster & Freeman, Ltd., manufactures the VSC 2000 microspectrophotometer with color space software, especially for document and ink analysis.

Test pens included roller-ball, fiber-tip, and ballpoint. The VSC2000 discriminated all black liquid inks tested, 89.74% of the blue liquid inks, 98.24% of the black non-liquid inks, and 90.90% of the blue non-liquid inks.

The Zeiss MPM discriminated all 182 pairs of black liquid and non-liquid ink, as well as over 98% of blue liquid and non-liquid ink. The MPM spectrum shows two blue roller-ball inks, which could be distinguished by none of the other methods, including VSC2000 spectrometer. No one non-destructive technique differentiated all inks tested, although the Zeiss MPM was close.

Visible Microspectrophotometry

An earlier series of cases using visible microspectrophotometry was reported by Larry Olson of the U.S. Immigration Forensic Document Laboratory.[4] He used a Nanospec 10S microspectrophotometer (380–900 nm range) with Leitz Orthoplan trinocular microscope. His procedure consisted of the following:

• Scan the paper background (% reflectance) from 400 to 700 nm.
• Set gain to 100% at wavelength of maximum reflectance.
• Scan again, store the spectrum in memory.
• Scan the ink sample and ratio with (subtract) stored background.
• Repeat the sample scan four additional times.

He reported tests of red inks that revealed slight differences in shape and relative peak height of spectral curves for different samplings of the same ink.

Ink opacity variations and micro-contamination, as well as paper interference can cause differences in microspectrophotometry spectra of the same inks. Also, multiple scans of the same ink can produce variations in spectra. In case studies, Olson successfully used microspectrophotometry for analysis of printed material, security fibers, and stamping inks. These inks could not be distinguished by visual inspection, and in the case of stamp ink, could not be distinguished by UV fluorescence. In each case, he differentiated counterfeit colored material from genuine and matched multiple questioned items with known spectra. He concluded that this technique could distinguish inks having different dye components, but he said that it could not be used to conclusively determine that inks contained the same components.

Sources of Interference in Visible Spectroscopy

Paper Interference

A study in 2000 by Linton Mohammed, James Buglio, and Anne-Marie Shafer of the San Diego Sheriff's Crime Laboratory reported little paper interference for visible range spectroscopy of inks performed with the VSC2000.[5]

Scattering and Bronzing Interference

Using a Nanometrics Docuspec TM/1 computerized microspectrophotometer with Olympus BHT microscope, Zeichner et al. reported lowered reproducibility of reflectance spectra with some inks, due to scatter and bronzing.[6]

Bronzing is a metallic-reddish microscopic appearance of ink when viewed with reflected light. Strongly absorbing inks will specularly reflect light of a color that is approximately complementary to light that the ink transmits.

Transmission spectra of the same ink may exhibit variations due to density variation of paper. To address this problem, these researchers deposited whole ink from a pen onto a polyethylene sheet. They then transferred this sample to a microscope slide and examined it in transmittance mode. They found that this mode eliminated the interference seen in the spectra. However, additional interference was present when the ink was allowed to dry. They also performed examination of single fibers and again found reproducibility low. Only fibers of non-tinted paper yielded acceptable spectra.

Zeichner and Glattstein,[7] in a later study, found that smearing inked fibers on a microscope slide with an engraving tool could reduce interference of the paper fiber in transmission microspectrophotometry. In some cases, a minute quantity of ink could be separated from the fiber onto the slide, permitting examination of pure ink. Two additional factors could influence spectra of the same ink: pressure applied with this smearing, and the drying time of the ink on the slide prior to smearing.

FOURIER TRANSFORM INFRARED SPECTROSCOPY (FTIR)

Whereas visible range spectroscopy measures color of a sample, infrared spectroscopy reveals specific features of a sample's molecular structure. FTIR can provide an absorbance "fingerprint" of a substance.

IR spectroscopy is based upon the ability of certain substances to absorb infrared radiation by interaction of an IR beam with a molecular bond of the analyte. Absorption occurs when the molecular bond has a vibrational frequency equal to (synchronous with) the IR beam. The wavelengths at which a measured absorption occurs correspond to particular functional groups.

A high-resolution method of measuring IR absorption, Fourier transform infrared spectroscopy, has today almost replaced the older, dispersive IR techniques.

FTIR uses a beam-splitter to create two source beams. A moving mirror changes the path difference between the two beams and produces an interference pattern. The computer then uses the mathematical process of Fourier transform to convert the time domain to frequency domain. FTIR gains a number of advantages over dispersive instruments, including higher resolution, higher signal-to-noise (S/N) ratios and greater throughput.

There are several sampling methods requiring different accessories or integrated instruments for FTIR, which have been investigated for ink analysis. Among these are Attenuated Total Reflectance (ATR) and Diffuse Reflectance (DRIFTS).

Attenuated Total Reflectance (ATR)

In ATR sampling, an optically dense crystal with a high refractive index is pressed against the sample. An IR beam is directed onto the crystal, turning the beam into an evanescent wave along the crystal. Each bounce of the wave penetrates the surface of the sample a distance measured in microns. The sample absorbs energy from the IR beam in regions characteristic of its functional groups and the IR beam exits the opposite end of the crystal. The instrument's detector analyzes the attenuated beam as an interference signal–from which an IR absorbance spectrum is generated. This sampling technique has been particularly promising for ink analysis since it can be performed with little or no destruction to the document. The shallow sampling depth can avoid penetration into the paper and thereby reduces paper interference. Depth of penetration of the IR beam is inversely proportional to the number of reflections and varies with the type of crystal material.[8]

ATR ANALYSIS OF BALLPOINT PEN INK. At the request of the authors, scientists at Nicolet Corporation performed analyses of ballpoint pen inks using the Nicolet Continuum Microscope ZnSe ATR. Figures 6.5 and 6.6 show distinctive IR spectra for two visually indistinguishable blue ballpoint inks. Previous tests had been conducted using a Nicolet Nexus FTIR spectrometer with ATR accessory. The latter instrument performed well for trace evidence materials; however, we encountered reproducibility problems when analyzing ink directly on paper.

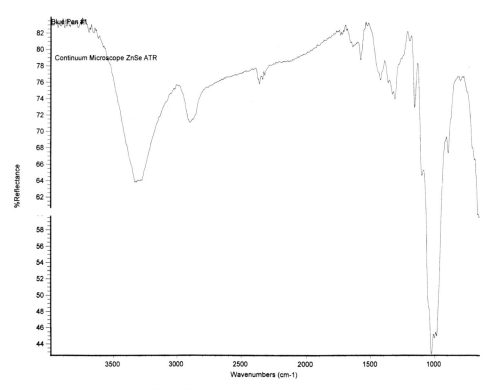

Figure 6.2. FTIR specturm–blue ballpoint pen ink 1.

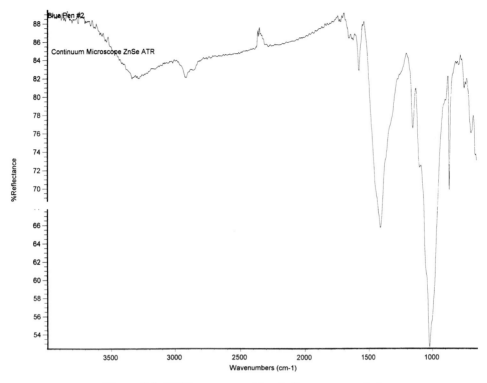

Figure 6.3. FTIR spectrum–blue ballpoint pen ink 2.

Diffuse Reflectance Infrared Spectroscopy (DRIFTS)

DRIFTS measures IR absorption of diffuse reflected light (light scattering in many directions). Preparation of an ink sample in a non-absorbing medium (e.g., KBr) minimizes spectral reflectance and increases depth of penetration into the sample. This, in turn, increases the contribution of the transmission and internal reflection components.

Rena Merrill and Edward Bartick differentiated some visibly indistinguishable ballpoint pen inks with DRIFTS. They used a Nicolet 20SXC FTIR spectrometer. In some cases they matched spectra with library standards.[9]

Procedure
- Remove 20 plugs of ink sample.
- Extract in 10 microliter pyridine for 30 minutes.
- Transfer 3 microliter extract to KBr DR Microsample cup.
- Use Spectra-Tech Collector DR accessory.

- Perform Scans: 256 with full aperture, 4000 to 650 cm^{-1}.
- Perform Subtractions: For residual CO_2 and H_2O.

These analysts created three libraries of 184 ballpoint inks: fresh ink, heated (artificially aged) ink, and extracted ink. Of 71 ballpoint inks, 38% matched the correct library ink formulation on the first hit for fresh ink. Another 42% correctly hit the correct ink from the library of heated inks. (Aged ink exhibits lower absorbance.) A correct first hit was achieved for 86% of 29 ink samples compared against the extracted ink library. An analyst trained in IR spectra interpretation examined the ink spectra to draw final conclusions.

In some samples, the paper contribution was 30% of the spectrum. They overcame this problem by paper blank subtraction. Also, the region from 4000 to 2000 cm^{-1} was "blanked" by a software routine to eliminate noise interference and absorbance variation in this region.

FTIR Comparison with TLC

Ink analysts use TLC to compare dyes. With FTIR you can also compare ink resins. Merrill and Bartick compared known FTIR absorption data with ink spectra and recognized IR features of specific known resins.

Resin Component	*Absorption Bands (Wavenumbers)*
Carbonyl (Ketone)	1705
Styrene-allyl alcohol copolymer	3090–3025, 1944, 1874, 1805, 1722, 1499, 750, 700

Pattern Recognition of FTIR Spectra

In 2001, a group of researchers, including Jian Wang of Tsinghua University, Beijing, published a method for comparison of FTIR spectra of blue ballpoint pen inks using statistical analysis to achieve pattern recognition of spectra.[10]

They used a Perkin-Elmer Spectrum 2000 FTIR Spectrometer and Auto Image Microscope with narrow band mercury cadmium telluride detector. Scanning over 4000 to 700 cm^{-1}, they found two broad groups of spectra among 108 samples, based upon absence or presence of absorption in the 2000 to 1700 cm^{-1} range.

They used a comparison of correlation coefficients between test samples (73 of the 108) and reference spectra (remaining 35 samples) to establish subgroups of ink samples. A correlation coefficient of 0.9800 or above generally indicted the same species. A lower value prompted comparison with the next reference spectrum–until satisfactory groupings were achieved. The first group (no absorption) was broken down into 6 subgroups, the second (strong absorption), into 29.

Analysis of Photocopier Toners with DRIFTS

In 1990, William Mazzella et al. successfully differentiated photocopier toners using DRIFTS.[11] They used both bulk toners and toner removed from the documents, examining the "fingerprint" IR range of 2100 to 700 cm^{-1}. Of 152 toners, 149 were classified into 36 groups based upon IR spectra. Neither the age of the toner nor latent print processing with ninhydrin affected the spectra.

Again, paper tends to be a significant contaminate when using this IR absorption technique. A method of sampling toner from a document which avoids paper contamination was described by James Brandi et al.[12] In this procedure, he clamped a section of toner-coated paper between microscope slides and heated it in a furnace at 200° C for 10 minutes. He then peeled the toner off the paper, onto the slide for examination.

Infrared Absorption Spectroscopy: Summary

Ink analysis by IR spectroscopy is complicated by a number of factors that are not generally a problem with visible range spectroscopy. Among these are paper interference and surface inhomogeneities. If these causes of unreliability can be overcome, IR absorption can differentiate visibly indistinguishable inks or presumptively identify an unknown. However, if infrared absorbance spectra are not definitive, another related technique can provide complementary information. That technique is Raman spectroscopy.

RAMAN SPECTROSCOPY

The Raman Effect, named for 1930 Nobel Laureate Sir Chandrasekhara Venkata ("C.V.") Raman of India, involves a "shift" in the wavelength of a small proportion of the light which is scattered upon irradiation of certain substances.[13] Because only about one excitation photon in 10^8–10^7 undergoes this shift, an intense irradiation source is needed.[14] Additionally, it must be monochromatic to measure the shift, thus, Raman spectroscopy uses a laser as an irradiation source. The scattered light is measured at some angle to the irradiation source, usually 90 degrees. "Elastic" or "Rayleigh" scattering occurs when the wavelength of the scattered light does not change from that of the irradiating energy.

If the wavelength of the scattered radiation changes, the scattering is said to be "inelastic." Inelastic scattering occurs as either a Stokes shift or anti-Stokes. A Stokes shift involves Raman scattered radiation in which the wavelength is longer than the irradiation source. Anti-Stokes Raman scattered radiation is shorter wavelength. Stokes shifts are more intense and are more commonly used in Raman spectroscopy. The magnitude of a Raman shift may be as much as 4000 cm^{-1} from the wavenumber of the irradiating laser beam.

Raman and FTIR both offer non-destructive, complementary information. FTIR provides greater sensitivity and is not impeded by fluorescence of the specimen. Raman often provides a very weak signal and may be masked by sample fluorescence (although some new modifications have addressed this limitation). Raman spectroscopy also has its advantages. Spectra are usually not as cluttered with peaks.[15] When used with a microscope, Raman can provide better sampling resolution, as small as 1 micron, as opposed to IR absorption which is limited to about 10 microns.[16]

Sample preparation is usually not required with Raman spectroscopy and paper substrate does not affect results.[17]

Raman's other advantages of permitting analysis through transparent containers and sampling through water, are of less interest to the ink analyst than to those using this technique in areas such as trace analysis. Raman works well with compounds having distributed electron clouds, e.g., carbon-carbon double bonds, a characteristic of many ink components. Raman spectra plot frequency shift (in wavenumbers) of irradiating light (abscissa) against relative intensity. It is dependent upon several factors, including, polarizability of the molecule, concentration of the species and the intensity of the source laser.[18]

Some laboratories have compiled libraries of Raman spectra of many substances of interest–including ink.

Raman spectroscopy and ballpoint pen ink

In 2000, Lyter reported Raman analysis of twelve black ballpoint inks. He compared its effectiveness with thin layer chromatography, as well as how complementary the two techniques would be in case-work.[19] The equipment and procedures were as follows:

- A Foster & Freeman Foram 685 Raman Spectrometer.
- 685 nm excitation wavelength with 1.0 mW laser power (Diode pumped Nd:YAG laser).
- Each ink sample was analyzed four times, each Raman line averaged five times.
- Thin layer chromatography involved use of "ATF I" solvent system.

Raman spectra divided the 12 black ballpoint pen ink samples into six distinct groups. One group, consisting of two ink samples, was featureless. Two more ink samples in one group exhibited fluorescence, making these four ink samples impossible to interpret. The best result of the Raman test was its ability to distinguish two very similar ink formulations. Raman could not differentiate between batches of the same ink formulation.

While Raman spectroscopy is non-destructive and thin layer chromatography is semi-destructive, TLC did differentiate all 12 ink formulations, whereas Raman could not. Examples of three unique spectra, spectra with small and absent features and fluorescent masking are illustrated in Figures 6.4–6.9.

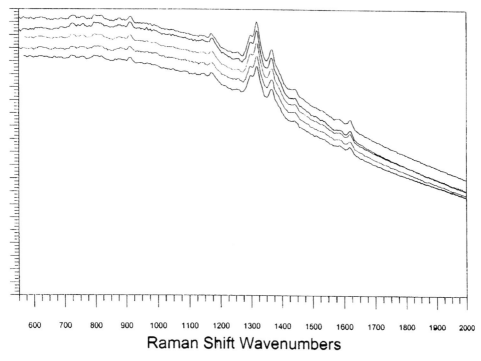

Raman Shift Wavenumbers

Figure 6.4. Black ballpoint 1–unique spectrum.

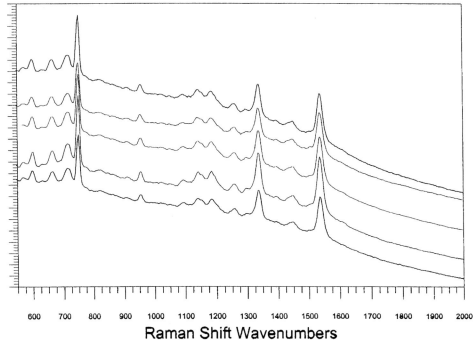

Figure 6.5. Black ballpoint 2–unique spectrum.

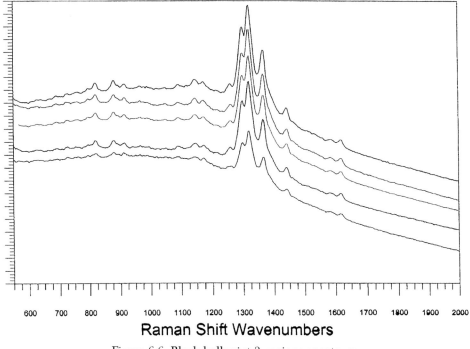

Figure 6.6. Black ballpoint 3–unique spectrum.

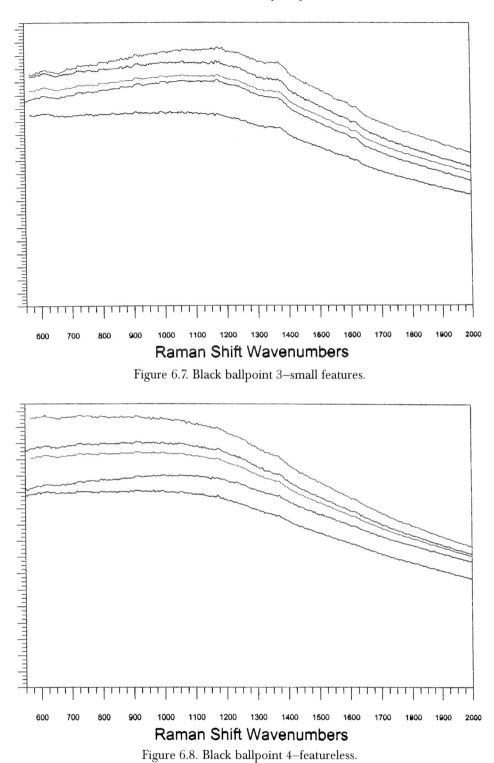

Figure 6.7. Black ballpoint 3–small features.

Figure 6.8. Black ballpoint 4–featureless.

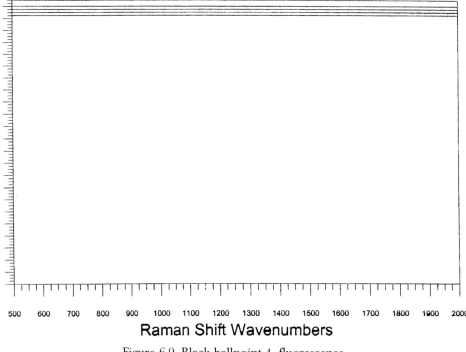

Figure 6.9. Black ballpoint 4–fluorescence.

New Methods of Ink Analysis by Raman Spectroscopy

Four types of Raman spectroscopy merit attention for ink analysis in coming years: Fourier transform, surface enhanced, resonance enhanced, and surface enhanced-resonance Raman spectroscopy. One advantage all offer for ink analysis is a reduction of fluorescent masking of the Raman signal. An additional recent innovation is the indium gallium arsenide (InGaAs) detector. This device features lower bandgap energy and is more sensitive in the near infrared than the CCD or photomultiplier tube (PMT) when using Nd:YAG or IR diode lasers.[20]

FT-RAMAN. Application of Fourier transform to Raman spectrometers permits use of a low-energy IR laser to excite the sample, minimizing fluorescence. FT Raman, like FTIR, also permits higher detection sensitivity.[21]

SURFACE ENHANCED RAMAN SPECTROSCOPY (SERS). The Raman effect is relatively weak, but it is enhanced by a factor of up to 14 orders of magnitude if the molecules of the sample are attached to—or within a few Angstroms—of metal particles. The effect is strongest for silver, but gold and copper can be used. Nakai and Nakatsuji[22] have shown that the electronic mechanism of SERS is due to the resonance transitions, involving surface polarization and the surface-molecule interaction. The enhancement is dependent upon surface-adsorbate orientation and separation distance. SERS of ink on paper is semi-destructive, requiring application of a solution of colloidal metal to the sample site.

RESONANCE-ENHANCED RAMAN SPECTROSCOPY. Resonance enhancement uses an excitation laser that lases at a wavelength that is within the electronic spectrum of the target molecule. This can increase Raman-active vibrations by two to four orders of magnitude. This form of Raman is especially useful for molecules that strongly absorb in the visible, a characteristic of ink dyes.

SURFACE ENHANCED RESONANCE RAMAN SPECTROSCOPY. A combination of the above-two Raman techniques often enhances the Raman effect to a greater degree than the enhancement of either procedure used independently. Foster & Freeman, Ltd., has recently introduced SERRS for ink analysis. This is in addition to their ordinary (Foram 685) Raman spectrometer. Wagner et al.[23] are currently researching this design for ink analysis.

At the University of Strathclyde, Glasgow, Scotland, as part of the Surface Enhanced Resonance Raman Scattering (SERRS) Project, Professor W. Ewen Smith and Dr. Peter C. White have studied SERRS in the analysis of small quantities of azo dyes.[24] They used silver as the surface enhancement metal and treated the silver with polylysine, so that the positively charged groups would bind to the charged azo compounds.

They reported that the Raman signals were very sharp and that it was easy to discriminate one molecule from another so that mixtures of dyes could be determined without further separation.

Resources on Raman Spectroscopy
- ASTM publication ASTM E 1840 shift standards for eight materials for calibrating Raman spectrometers
- *The Internet Journal of Vibrational Spectroscopy*
- *The Journal of Raman Spectroscopy*

HIGH-PERFORMANCE LIQUID CHROMATOGRAPHY

Liquid chromatography, like TLC, uses a solid stationary phase and a liquid mobile phase. The principle differences are that LC uses a column to contain the stationary packing, a pump to transport the solvent, and a detector to produce a spectrum of the separated samples.

The form of LC used today for analysis (as opposed to mere separation) is "High-Performance" LC (which has also been termed "High Pressure"), with the same acronym. Like HPTLC, *High-Performance* liquid chromatography uses smaller particles in the stationary phase, which produces greater column efficiency. In its column packing, high-performance liquid chromatography uses many of the same sorbents used on thin layer chromatography plates. Solvent choices for liquid chromatography can often be made quickly and easily by first testing samples with high-performance, thin layer chromatography. HPLC is particularly useful for separating thermally fragile, non-volatile substances, including high molecular weight molecules. For ink analysis, HPLC generally offers greater sensitivity than HPTLC and better separation of dyes.[25] HPLC equipment includes:

- A reservoir into which the mobile phase (liquid) is placed.
- A pump, which forces the liquid phase through the system.
- An injector, where sample analytes are introduced.
- A separation column where the chromatographic partitioning and separation of the components of the sample take place.
- A detector for analyzing the separated components as they emerge from the column in the effluent (and/or a fraction collector for capturing the separated components).

Common detectors are mass spectrometers, and fluorescence or absorbance spectrometers. For ink analysis, the latter are most useful when multiwavelength detectors are used.

Non Ballpoint Pen Ink Differentiation by HPLC

Ian Tebbett et al. distinguished 108 of 113 blue non-ballpoint pen inks using HPLC equipped with a multiwavelength detector.[26] By contrast, they found that TLC could only separate this set of inks into 17 groups. These inks were distinguishable by UV but not visible absorbance. The effectiveness of UV was due to the UV absorbing properties of ink vehicles. In contrast to these findings, the authors have been able to discriminate all non-ballpoint inks using TLC combined with densitometry.

Equipment
- Perkin Elmer Series 3B LC pump, 20 μl loop.
- Column Spherisorb 5 μm ODS.
- Optimum Mobile phase—acetonitrile:water (80:20) with 0.005M Heptane sulphonic acid, pH 4.7.
- Flow rate: 1 mL/minute.
- Detector monitoring: 200–800 nm.

Procedure
- Ink Samples: 5 mm X 1 mm ink-soaked paper (Single handwritten comma or period is sufficient).
- Ink extraction: Sonicated 20 minutes in LC mobile phase solvent.
- Ink Sample Injected: 20 μl.

Two distinguishable HPLC chromatograms of non ballpoint blue inks using multiwavelength detection (UV) are illustrated in Figures 6.10 and 6.11.

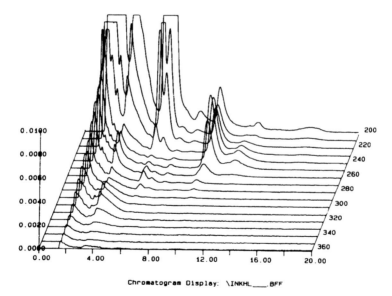

Chromatogram Display: \INKHL___.BFF

Figure 6.10. HPLC chromatogram of blue non-ballpoint ink 1. Courtesy of *Journal of Forensic Sciences.*

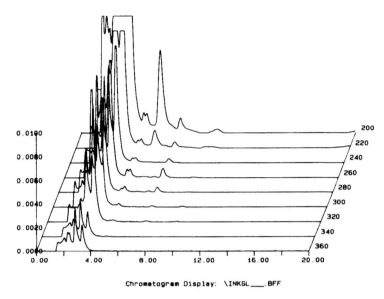

Figure 6.11. HPLC chromatogram of blue non-ballpoint ink 2. Courtesy of *Journal of Forensic Sciences.*

Supercritical Fluid Extraction

Tebbett[27] has used this alternate means of ink extraction prior to LC analysis. SFE involves using a supercritical gas as an ink solvent. In this technique, the gas (usually CO_2) is maintained above its critical pressure and temperature. This supercritical form is intermediate between a gas and a liquid. It dissolves the ink in a manner similar to use of organic solvents, but with the diffusion rate of a gas.

Black Ballpoint Pen Ink Differentiation by HPLC

T.D. Whiting, in 1998, tested a procedure that used HPLC to differentiate four black ballpoint inks.[28]

Equipment
- Injector system: Waters 712 Wisp Millepore, model 510 pumps.
- Column: Waters Nova Pak C–18, 2 mm X 150 mm.
- Mobile phase: 100 mM Acetonitrile/Potassium Phosphate buffer with 50:50 to 95:5 gradient.
- pH 3.2.

Sonicate a 40 mm ink line in 100 µl mobile phase solvent 25 minutes and centrifuge 30 minutes, prior to injection.

Whiting compared the HPLC results to capillary electrophoresis. Both techniques differentiated ballpoint inks; however, he suggests CE may be preferable. This is because CE uses aqueous buffers, not solvents, features lower column replacement and consumables cost, and requires smaller samples.

Evaluation of HPLC Data by Pattern Recognition Methods

In 2001, Kher, Green, and Mulholland[29] reported the use of pattern recognition methods (derived from HPLC data) for writing ink differentiation. These methods may be applied to data of virtually any type of instrumental analysis.

For PCA (principle components analysis) they used Sirius 6.52 software to analyze max plots (three-dimensional chromatograms). This software uses a cross-validation algorithm that creates score plots. These are graphical clusters that summarize chromatographic data in a form you can readily compare by graphical separation distances. Two ink samples with a separation distance of less than one are not discriminated; 1-3 means some discrimination; over three indicates a satisfactory discrimination.

A second pattern recognition technique is flow chart classification. Here, the analyst makes stepwise differentiation decisions on the basis of presence or absence of a chromatographic peak at a particular retention time or wavelength/retention. This group tabulated percentiles for differentiation of known standard inks at detection wavelengths of 254, 279, 370, and 400 nm. The majority of inks tested, from Uniball, Zebra, Pilot, and Bic ballpoints, could be discriminated or identified. Detection at 370 was most effective for blue ballpoint ink, which was also more easily discriminated than black.

They suggest development of an ink database for use in forensic ink classification and discrimination, possibly including mass spectrometry.

ELECTROPHORESIS

Electrophoresis is an analytical technique in which components of a mixture are introduced into a buffer and subjected to a high-voltage electric field. This field induces migration and separation. The different relative migration rates are owing to differences in size and/or net charge of the molecules. Whereas thin layer chromatography produces a chromatogram or separation pattern of the components of a mixture, electrophoresis produces an electropherogram. In paper or slab-gel electrophoresis, the electropherogram resembles a thin layer chromatogram. In capillary electrophoresis, a detector and spectrometer analyze the migrating components, and the CE electropherogram is a series of spectra.

One modification of capillary electrophoresis, called micellar electrokinetic capillary chromatography, has proven to be particularly useful for ballpoint ink analysis. In this technique, a surfactant is added to the buffer and differences in migration rates are due, in part, to differential partitioning within a micellar pseudostationary phase.

Electrophoresis Categories and Comparisons

Paper Electrophoresis

The earliest form of this technique, paper electrophoresis, uses a cellulose acetate strip as a migration medium.

Slab-Gel Electrophoresis

The sieving medium is a slab of porous gel, e.g., polyacrylamide.

Capillary Electrophoresis

Component separation is achieved in a capillary tube (inside diameter ca. 10–100 microns). The advantages of CE over slab-gel are that capillary electrophoresis:
1. Is faster and easier equipment set up and operation.
2. Features automation capabilities.
3. Requires smaller sample size.
4. Produces less waste, thus smaller disposal problems of gel and eluent.
5. Permits use of real-time detectors for analysis of separated components.
6. Accommodates use of higher voltages due to higher surface area-to-volume ratio of the buffer/gel.[30]

Capillary electrophoresis is generally thought to have advantages over TLC/HPTLC in that it is more discriminating, offers higher resolving power and generally requires smaller sample (unless using direct elution in TLC). However, most ink chemists still prefer using HPTLC.

OPEN TUBE CAPILLARY ELECTROPHORESIS. The capillary contains no gel matrix, only buffer solution. Separation of analytes is achieved by their different charge-to-mass ratios. There are currently two sub-categories, which we will examine:

MICELLAR ELECTROKINETIC CAPILLARY ELECTROPHORESIS (MECE). Also called Micellar Electrokinetic Capillary Chromatography (MECC) or Micellar Electrokinetic Chromatography (MEKC). This technique involves adding a surfactant e.g., sodium dodecylsulfate (SDS) to the buffer. The surfactant forms micelles (colloidal particles resulting from ionic aggregation) which remain in suspension. The micelles form a "pseudostationary phase," similar to the stationary phase of true chromatographic techniques. This micelle formation increases the solubility of water-insoluble (hydrophobic) species. Upon application of the electric field, the analytes undergo differential partitioning (an equilibrium distribution ratio) amongst the micelles. This results in different relative migration times, affected by their differing interaction with the micelles.

Micelle formation from buffer application in MECE works well for component separation of analytes of low water solubility–such as ballpoint pen ink.

CAPILLARY ZONE ELECTROPHORESIS (CZE). Capillary Zone Electrophoresis is also called "Free-Zone CE" or "High-Performance CE." (Note: In slab-gel electrophoresis "CZE" has been used for "Continuous-Zone Electrophoresis.")

PHYSICAL GEL CE. This is a CE technique in which a hydrophilic polymer solution is pumped into the capillary and pumped out after each run.

CHEMICAL GEL CE. In chemical gel CE, the solution and catalyst is pumped into the capillary where it polymerizes into a sieve gel matrix. The gel is not removable.

Capillary Electrophoresis Variable Parameters

In each CE procedure, the analyst must determine and adjust variable parameters. These include the following:

Electrolyte:
- Ionic strength

- Organic solvent additives
- pH additives
- Micellar additives

Capillary:
- Material type
- Total length
- Length to detector
- Inner and outer diameter
- Zeta potential

Equipment:
- Applied voltage
- Polarity
- Injection volume (pressure and time)
- Operating temperature cooling mechanism
- Detector type
- Detection range

Electrophoresis Procedures Used in Ink Analysis

Paper Electrophoresis

Wilson Harrison discussed paper electrophoresis in his 1957 *Suspect Documents*.[31] Most ink analysts regard paper electrophoresis (like paper chromatography) of historical interest only—since the development of newer, more discriminating methods.

Slab-gel Electrophoresis

The only reference found in the literature applying this technique to pen ink was H. L. Moon in 1980.[32] He used an agarose gel plate for analysis of fiber tip pen inks. Moon placed 3 mm lines of ink into slots the same length in the center of the plate. The best separation occurred at 200 V for 8 minutes.

High-Performance Capillary Electrophoresis of Ballpoint Pen Ink

Whiting compared high-performance capillary electrophoresis (Capillary Zone CE) with high-performance liquid chromatography (HPLC) in the analysis of 1988 and 1989 formulab black, Paper-Mate

Flexgrip, and PM-39 Bic ballpoint pen inks.[33] Both techniques differentiated the four samples. The HPCE method provided consistent results with sample sizes as small as 5 mm of ink line. Such a small sampling is important because this may be all the sample available in the region of the ink entries to be compared in an actual forensic ink analysis problem.

He used a Beckman P/ACE System 5500 with UV detector set at 200 nm. The capillary consisted of a Beckman electrophoresis uncoated fused silica cartridge, 60 cm length, 50 micron i.d., a buffer of 100 mM, 1:1 Acetonitrile/Potassium Phosphate, pH 3.2, maintaining the buffer at 25° C. The operating voltage was 25 kV.

Procedure
- Place ink line in 50 μl buffer, transfer to ultrasonic bath 25 minutes, then centrifuge for 30 minutes. In tests to date, the minimum effective amount of sample for extraction was a 5 mm ink line.
- Pressure inject sample extract for 20 seconds. Optimum run time has been determined to be 15 minutes.

Micellar Electrokinetic Capillary Chromatography of Ballpoint Pen Ink

X. Xu, J.A. de Koeijer, J.J. M. de Moel, and H. Logtenberg, at the Ministry of Justice, Forensic Science Laboratory, The Netherlands, have successfully used Micellar Electrokinetic Capillary Chromatography (MECC) to differentiate ballpoint pen inks. They could not differentiate these inks by HPTLC or HPLC.[34] Their procedure produced good dye separation, regardless of molecular charge since they theorize, separation is based primarily upon molecular size.

The CE instrument used by this group was a Beckman P/ACE 5500 CE system with a polyimide-coated fused silica capillary of 50 microns i.d.

Procedure
- Prepare and equilibrate the separation solution for three days prior to use. The solution consists of 70% buffer and 30% co-solvent.
- Prepare the separation solution by combining buffer and acetonitrile (70:30).
- Buffer is prepared from: 60 mM sodium dodecyl sulphate (SDS),

with 0.5 mM. Brij-35, 15 mM of 3-amino-1-propanol and 7.5 mM HCl.

- Extract each ink micro plug in 0.5 µl 2(2-methoxyethoxy) ethanol in sealed micro-vials for 5 minutes in an ultrasonic bath.
- Dilute the extract with ca. 1 microliter of 2 mM Brij-35.
- Pressure inject this extract into the instrument capillary at 0.5 psi for 4 seconds.
- Use applied potential of +30 kV(72 µA) for 30 minutes (57 cm capillary length) or +25 kV(76 µA) for 47 cm.
- Set diode array detector for 200–600 nm, with 4 nm bandwidth.

SEPARATION TIME REPRODUCIBILITY. Over 24 runs, the relative standard deviation was 0.66%. This group determined that changes over time indicted evaporation of acetonitrile, thus, they suggest changing the buffer every five hours.

ELECTROPHEROGRAMS. They found the same ink dye components can produce multiple UV-absorbing peaks, or baselines. This indicates different sources or ages of the same compounds—or differences in the paper upon which the sampled ink lines were written. The best tool for differentiation was comparison of the area ratios of the separated sub-peaks of the identical dyes of different samples. Figures 6.12 and 6.13 show distinguishable electropherograms of two ballpoint pen inks, with detection at 215 nm and 570 nm in each. The labeling on the electropherograms corresponds to peaks for the following: M Methyl violet, Sb Solvent Blue 38, Bg background, U unknown.

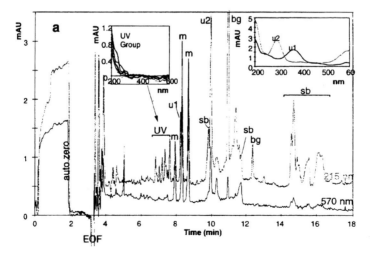

Figure 6.12. Parker medium blue ballpoint ink. Courtesy of *International Journal of Forensic Document Examiners.*

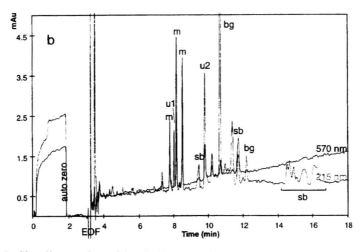

Figure 6.13. Sheaffer medium blue ballpoint ink. Courtesy of International *Journal of Forensic Document Examiners.*

One caution should be noted: Samples cannot be differentiated based upon differences in absolute concentration values of peaks. They theorize that this is due to ink differences in component concentration at different points along the written line.

QUALITY CONTROL. Flush the capillary. Ballpoint ink components can adsorb to the capillary wall. This group uses an HCl-MeOH-NaOH-H_2O buffer in the flushing cycle.

Capillary Zone Electrophoresis of Ballpoint Pen Ink

Carla Vogt, Andreas Becker, and Jurgen Vogt, at The University of Leipzig, have conducted extensive research on analysis of dyes, resins, and metals in ballpoint pen ink.[35]

Equipment

For this procedure, they used a Beckman P/ACE 2100 with fused silica capillaries, i.d. 50 microns, 77 cm length, and a Perkin Elmer-Applied Biosystems Model 270A-HAT equipped with fused silica capillaries, i.d. 50 microns, 70 cm length.

Procedure

• Add organic modifiers (e.g., 50% acetonitrile) to buffer solutions containing SDS. At this level, formation of micelles is inhibited; thus the procedure is not MECC. Instead, the non-ionic portions of the analytes (in this case dyes) interact with the surfactants, while the ionic portions interact with the aqueous buffer solution.

- Use either of two CE buffers. The best separation was achieved with 50 mM borate, pH 9.0 and 50% acetonitrile. A faster (but possibly less satisfactory separation) is achieved without a surfactant using the same buffer system, but adding 30 mM SDS.
- Prepare samples by removing 10 plugs of a ballpoint ink line and extract in 50 microliters of the above-modified buffer solution.
- Introduce samples by 5, 8, and 10-second hydrodynamic injection. Use operating voltage of 15 and 25 kV.

UV/VIS ABSORBANCE. Detection was provided by diode array, which scans from 190 to 600 nm, with absorbance executed at 205 nm.

LASER-INDUCED FLUORESCENCE. An excitation wavelength of 320 nm was produced by an Omnichrom Series 74 He-Cd Laser (27 mW), scanning 200–600 nm. Fluorescence was detected at 405 nm.

RESIN ANALYSIS BY CE. The Leipzig group attempted to analyze ballpoint pen ink resins by CE using a sieving gel medium. However, they reported that resins appear to be too tightly bound to paper to permit satisfactory extraction and analysis. Resin extraction and analysis from a written ballpoint pen ink line is an ongoing area of research.

Capillary Zone Electrophoresis of Water-Soluble Fiber Tip Pen Ink

In 1991, Salvatore Fanali of Italy and Martin Schudel of Switzerland published a study of CZE applied to the analysis of water-soluble, fiber-tip pen inks. They analyzed ink samples taken directly from pens and ran CZE analysis of extracts from faint TLC spots of those same inks (adding the latter to whole ink samples).[36] This procedure provided a means of matching components separated through TLC with electropherogram peaks.

They used a Bio-Rad HPE 100 with UV detector set at 206 nm, operating at 12 kV, with positive charge at the detector. The chosen coated capillary was 20 cm by 0.025 mm. The buffer solution was a 3:1 mixture of 0.1 M ammonium acetate (pH 4.5) and methanol.

Capillary Zone Electrophoresis of Fountain Pen Inks

In a study published in 1997, Ellen Rohde, William R. Heineman, and Annette C. McManus, of the University of Cincinnati Department of Chemistry, along with Carla Vogt, of the University of Leipzig, distinguished 15 blue and black fountain pen ink samples by their electropherograms.[37]

In tests comparing whole ink vs. the same ink extracted from a written line on paper, differences were detected in the electropherograms. This was probably due to differences in extraction efficiency of the ink components in the extraction solution (ultrasonic extraction in ethanol and water, 1:1). As in all attempts to identify the make of pen ink through comparison of extracts with whole samples, this difference should be noted.

Equipment

A Beckman model P/ACE 5510 with UV/VIS diode array detector (set at 214 nm) was equipped with fused silica capillaries of 50 micron i.d, of lengths of 37 and 57 inches.

Procedure

- Prepare a 50 mM borate buffer at pH 8.0. A second separation procedure uses phosphate buffer at pH 8.0.
- Set potential for +25 kV.
- To extract, sonicate 6 micro plugs in 50 μl of EtOH and H_2O, 1:1 for 15 minutes.
- Hydrodynamically inject 32 s for blue ink; 16 s for black.

These researchers suggest that using their instrumentation, pre-concentration of the injected analyte may be necessary to avoid overlong injection. Otherwise, the procedure can result in loss of signal intensity in the electropherogram.

Summary

Capillary electrophoresis is a highly effective means of analyzing ink from a variety of writing instrument categories. The limitation of CE is that it does not permit parallel analysis, that is, you cannot compare two inks simultaneously.

Additional Separation Techniques

The LC and CE techniques described above are only a few of the possible variations that might have applications in ink analysis. Others include pressurized electrochromatography and its high performance version, electro-HPLC. There are many more separation technologies, which have not been tried for ink analysis, and new techniques are continually being developed.

Resources

The Journal of Capillary Electrophoresis

MASS SPECTROMETRY

Theory

Mass Spectrometry measures the mass of atoms, molecules or fragments of molecules, and the relative abundance of each. The analyte is ionized and introduced into the mass spectrometer, which uses magnetic and electric fields to exert forces on the charged particles (ions) in a vacuum. The mass spectrum shows the mass to charge ratio (m/e) as the horizontal component and the relative intensity (relative abundance of each ion) as the peak height. The highest peak is the "base peak" and serves as the reference (usually equivalent to 100) for measuring the relative abundance of all other ions present in the spectrum.

Some of the current methods of mass spectrometry ionization include gas-phase ionization, chemical ionization (CI), negative-ion chemical ionization, electron ionization (EI), desorption chemical ionization (DCI), field desorption and ionization, field desorption (FD), field ionization (FI), secondary ion mass spectrometry (SIMS), fast atom bombardment (FAB), atmospheric pressure ionization, electrospray ionization (ESI), atmospheric pressure chemical ionization (APCI), and matrix-assisted laser desorption ionization (MALDI).

In Chapter 9, we discuss a procedure for dating inks by analyzing the volatile components by gas chromatography combined with mass spectrometry (GC-MS) using electron impact ionization. Since most of the volatile components evaporate rapidly from ink that has dried on paper, this technique is of limited usefulness for ink differentiation. Also, many ink components are not gaseous and are heat labile. This requires that the analyst use a different method to introduce ink samples into the mass spectrometer. One type of mass spectrometry that analysts have used successfully for ink differentiation is field desorption.

Field Desorption Mass Spectrometry (FDMS)

In FDMS, the emitter is a wire bearing hundreds of carbon microtips or fine crystalline "whiskers." The analyst removes the emitter from the instrument and coats it with a solution of the ink sample, reinserting it into the instrument. The analyst then applies a high potential (usually several kilovolts) to the emitter. This creates a high voltage electric field near the tips of the whiskers, at which point ionization and evaporation of the analyte occurs.

Field desorption is a "soft" ionization method, i.e., it produces little ion excitation and yields spectra which seldom include fragment-ions. This means that you will typically see one molecule or molecular ion per compound. This can preclude distinction of different ink dye compounds, which have the same molecular weight–but different molecular structure (as seen in the first procedure below.) A plus for field desorption is that it works well for organometallics (which characterizes some ink dyes). It is overall less sensitive than "hard" MS methods, such as electron impact; however, it can yield considerable information compared to other techniques commonly used for ink analysis.

A procedure for analysis of basic ballpoint pen inks by field desorption mass spectrometry was reported in 1999 by Masataka Sakayanagi and colleagues at the Scientific Criminal Investigation Laboratory, Yokohama Japan.[38]

Instrument
- JOEL JMS-AX505HA magnetic sector mass spectrometer.
- Probe/instrument tuning: m/z 58 ion of acetone generated by FDMS.

Procedure
Apply samples (1 mm ink line, extracted in methanol) to the carbon FDMS emitter. Use following instrument settings:
- Acceleration potential: 3 kV.
- Cathode voltage: – 5 kV.
- Source temperature: $25°C$ (no heating).
- Emitter current sweep: 0-40 mA @ 2 mA/minute.

Mass calibration is performed with an Ultramark 1621, fast atom bombardment ionization.

Results

This group achieved differentiation of black ballpoint pen inks and red ballpoint pen inks by identification and comparison of basic dyes present. They had previously compiled a library containing chemical information on dyes that they were likely to encounter. Figures 6.14 and 6.15 show mass spectra of dyes basic blue 26 and basic violet 1. These constituents can be seen in the mass spectrum for a blue ballpoint pen ink (Figure 6.16).

The only complication they encountered was the inability of FDMS to differentiate different compounds of the same molecular weight. This was true of the dyes Basic Violet 10 and Basic Red 1, which both have a molecular weight of 443.

Basic Violet 1 is sold as a mixture of three homologues of molecular weights 372, 358, and 344. It is present in one spectrum, with 372 representing the base peak. Nuclear Magnetic Resonance spectra confirmed that this was in fact the most abundant homologue.

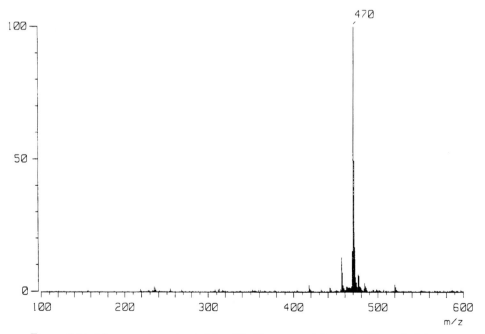

Figure 6.14. Mass spectrum basic blue 26. Courtesy of *Journal of Forensic Sciences.*

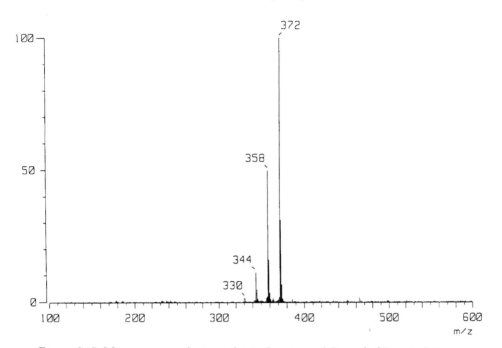

Figure 6.15. Mass spectrum basic violet 1. Courtesy of *Journal of Forensic Sciences.*

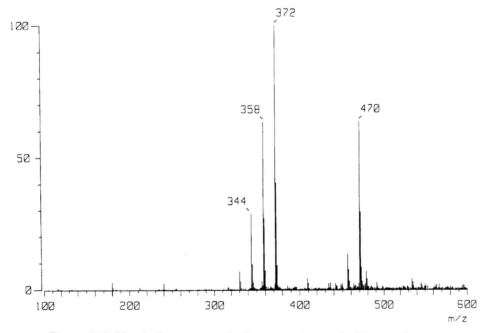

Figure 6.16. Blue ballpoint pen ink. Courtesy of *Journal of Forensic Sciences.*

These researchers suggest that FDMS is useful for ink differentiation as well as for identification of pen manufacturer. This determination is based upon the relative abundance of specific dyes found to be present, compared to a previously established database.

Electron Impact Mass Spectrometry in Identification of Dye-Pack

As mentioned in Chapter 3, dye-pack is a bank security device. It is placed within a stolen money container whereupon it bursts, expelling tear gas and spreading a red dye, marking the currency as stolen. Because the evidence involves a dye on paper, analysis of stained currency may be directed to the crime laboratory's ink analyst.

Identification of a red stain produced by dye-pack requires detection of 1-methylaminoanthraquinone (MAAQ) in the stains. This dye can be detected by GC-MS, using electron impact (and possibly other) sample ionization techniques. Dyes other than MAAQ may be present; thus, finding another dye does not preclude the possibility that a red stain may be Dye-Pack.[39] If a red dye is UV fluorescent or it is insoluble in acetone and toluene, it is not MAAQ.

You may also be asked to determine whether Dye-Pack stains have been removed from currency. Seiden[40] suggests testing for the following:

- Acidic pH.
- An absence of colored fibers in portions of the note.
- Worn and discolored or pinkish appearance.
- Odor of hydrogen sulfite.
- Scorch marks from the exploding device.

Since it is peripheral to the subject of this book, we will not go into Dye-Pack analysis detail here; however, if you are called upon to perform this procedure, you are advised to confer with the FBI laboratory for assistance and recommendations. The procedure for submitting suspected dye-pack stained currency to the FBI is explained in the *FBI Handbook of Forensic Services: Evidence Examinations–Bank Security Dyes.* That publication can be found on the FBI website.

Additional methods of ink analysis by mass spectrometry, which are being investigated for ink dating, are described in Chapter 9.

What Is the Best Technique for Ink Comparison?

You can potentially show that two inks are definitely of different chemical formulations using any technique described in this book–so long as you follow proper procedure and you bear in mind the technique's limitations.

Some techniques will predictably differentiate a greater percentage of the inks than will other techniques. A rule of thumb is: Try all fast non-destructive techniques available to you first.

Of the semi-destructive techniques, at this time we believe the best combination for performance, economy and simplicity remains high-performance thin layer chromatography. HPLC and capillary electrophoresis may be more discriminating than HPTLC; however, the initial equipment investment is far higher and, unlike HPTLC, the latter two techniques do not permit parallel (side-by-side) analysis of samples.

A combination of techniques that measures different chemical parameters will provide corroborative evidence that two formulations are identical. The rarer the pen that the formulations match, the greater the evidentiary significance. However, as we've said, even if you prove to a scientific certainty that two formulations are chemically identical, you are still unable to say that the same pen was used to make both written entries–unless you know that the pen associated with that ink formulation is unique.

One example of such a product, albeit not one you will likely encounter in casework, is the *DNA Pen*, from DNA Technologies, Inc.[41] Ink from this pen is combined with the owner's DNA, and its writing can presumably be matched with the pen that produced it–with the conclusiveness of forensic DNA testing.

REFERENCES

1. Kerr, L. K.: Objective comparison of ball-point inks via multivariant statistical analysis of complementary chromaticity coordinates derived from visible microspectrophotometric data–A preliminary report. Presented at the 45th annual meeting of the American Academy of Forensic Sciences.
2. Seipp, U.: Applications of UV/VIS microspectrophotometry and microspectrofluorimetry in document examination. *Int. J. Forensic Document Examiners*, 3/1: 14–30, Jan/Mar., 1997.

3. Josey, L., Oroku, K. G. & Tanaka, T.: Honolulu Police Department Crime Laboratory: Measuring the effectiveness of non-destructive examination of inks utilizing macroscopic/microscopic, infrared, infrared luminescence and ultraviolet techniques and instrumentation. Presented at the 52nd annual meeting the American Academy of Forensic Sciences.

4. Olson, L. A.: Color comparison in questioned document examination using microspectrophotometry. *JFS*, 31/4: 1330–1340, Oct. 1986.

5. Mohammed, L., Buglio, J. & Shafer, A.: San Diego Sheriff's Crime Laboratory: The influence of paper on the performance of the VSC-2000 spectrometer. Presented at the 58th Annual Meeting of the American Society of Questioned Document Examiners.

6. Zeichner, A., Levin, N., Klein, A. & Novoselky, Y.: Transmission and reflectance microspectrophotometry of inks. *JFS*, 33/5:1171–1184, Sept. 1988.

7. Zeichner, A. & Glattstein, B.: Some special observations regarding visible transmission spectra of inks and an improved method for their discrimination by microspectrophotometry. *JFS*, 37/3, May, 1992.

8. Nicolet Corporation, Smart accessory data, 2000.

9. Merrill, R. & Bartick, E.: Analysis of ballpoint pen inks by diffuse reflectance IR spectrometry. *JFS* 37/2, March, 1992.

10. Wang J., Luo, G., Sun, S. & Wang. Y.: Systematic analysis of bulk blue ballpoint pen ink by FTIR spectrometry. *JFS* 2001;46(5):1093–1097.

11. Mazzella, W. D., Lennard, C. J. & Margot, P. A.: Classification and identification of photocopying toners by diffuse reflectance infrared Fourier transform spectroscopy (DRIFTS): II. Final Report. *JFS*, 36/3, May, 1991.

12. Brandi, J., James, B. & Gutowski, S. J.: Differentiation and classification of photocopier toners. *Int. J. Forensic Document Examiners*, 3/4: 324–343, Oct/Dec. 1997.

13. Ferraro, J. R. & Kakamoto, K.: *Introductory Raman Spectroscopy;* 1994.

14. Tedesco, J.: Kaiser Optical Systems: *Laser Focus World*, p. 161, September, 2000.

15. Skoog, D. A.: *Principles of Instrumental Analysis.* p. 306, Saunders College Publishing, 1971.

16. Bowden, M. & Gardiner, D. J.: Department of Chemical and Life Sciences, University of Northumbria at Newcastle, Ellison Place, Newcastle upon Tyne, UK, NE1 8ST.; IJVS 2:2, 2000.

17. See 15 above (p. 303).

18. Gilchrist, J. R., Rebello, J., Lanzisera, D. & Noonan, J.: Indium gallium arsenide detectors open up the near-IR. *Laser Focus World*, pp. 149–156, May, 2000.

19. Lyter, A. H. III: A comparative analysis of ball pen ink by Raman spectroscopy and thin layer chromatography. Presented at the 52nd Annual Meeting of the American Academy of Forensic Sciences, February 2000.

20. See 14 above.

21. National Renewable Energy Laboratory, The National Center for Photovoltaics: *Measurements and Characterization*, 1999.

22. Nakai, H. & Nakatsuji, H.: Electronic mechanism of the surface enhanced Raman scattering. *J. Chem. Phys*, Vol. 103, No. 6: 2286–2294, 1995.

23. Wagner, E., Burke, N., Clement, S. & Foster, D.: Preliminary results of surface

enhanced resonance Raman (SERRS). Presentation at the Annual Meeting of the American Society of Questioned Document Examiners, 2000.

24. Hunro, C. H., White, P. C. & Smith, W. E.: The use of poly-L-lysine and ascorbic acid for the SERRS analysis of acid mono-azo dyes. *Analyst* 118:731–733, 1993.

25. Tebbett, I. R., Chen, C., Fitzgerald, M. & Olson, L.: The use of HPLC with multiwavelength detection for the differentiation of non ball pen inks. *JFS*, 37/4: 1149–1157, July, 1992.

26. Ibid.

27. National Institute of Justice Research Brief, P. 14, August, 1996.

28. Whiting, T. D.: Discrimination of ballpoint pen inks by high performance capillary electrophoresis and high performance liquid chromatography. *Journal of the American Society of Questioned Document Examiners*, p. 12, June 1998.

29. Kherr, A. A., Green, E. V. & Mulholland, M. I.: Evaluation of principal components analysis with high-performance liquid chromatography and photodiode array detection for the forensic differentiation of ballpoint pen inks. *JFS*, 46/4: 878–883.

30. Landers, J. P.: *Handbook of Capillary Electrophoresis.* 1997, p. 351–353.

31. Harrison, W.: *Suspect Documents.* p.124, Frederick A. Praeger, 1958.

32. Moon, H. W.: Electrophoretic identification of felt tip pen inks. *JFS*, 25/1: 146–149, Jan. 1980.

33. Whiting, T. D.: Discrimination of ballpoint pen inks by high performance capillary electrophoresis and high performance liquid chromatography. *Journal of the American Society of Questioned Document Examiners*, 1/1:12–16, June, 1998.

34. Xu, X., de Koeijer, J. A., de Moel, J. J. M. & Logtenberg, H.: Ink analysis for forensic science applications by micellar electrokinetic capillary chromatography with photo-diode array detection. *Int. J. Forensic Document Examiners*, 3/3:240–260, July/Sept. 1997.

35. Vogt, C., Becker, A. & Vogt, J.: Investigation of ball point pen inks by capillary electrophoresis (CE) with UV/Vis absorbance and laser induced fluorescence detection and particle induced x-ray emission (PIXE). *JFS*, 44/4: 819–831, 1999.

36. Fanali, S. & Schudel, M.: Some separation of black and red water-soluble fiber-tip pen inks by capillary zone electrophoresis and thin-layer chromatography. *JFS*, 36/4:1192–1197, July 1991.

37. Rohde, E., Heineman, W., McManus, A. & Vogt, C.: Separation and comparison of fountain pen inks by capillary zone electrophoresis. *JFS*, 42/6:1004–1011, 1997.

38. Sakayanagi, M., Pharm, B., Komuro, J., Konda, Y., Watanabe, K. & Harigaya, Y.: Analysis of ballpoint pen inks by field desorption mass spectrometry. *JFS*, 44/6: 1204–1214, 1999.

39. Personal correspondence with FBI Laboratory, 4/20/98.

40. Seiden, H.: Removal of dye-pack stains on U.S. currency: A reconstruction. *Int. J. Forensic Document Examiners*, 2/3:220–225, July/Sept 1996.

41. DNA Technologies Inc., Los Angeles, California; www.dnatechnologies.com, 2000.

Chapter 7

INK LIBRARIES

Identification of a specific ink formulation requires access to a comprehensive collection of ink standards. Ideally, these standards should be obtained directly from the ink manufacturers because it is they who can best provide information about their inks. This information should include: (1) the manufacturer of the ink, (2) the formulation number of the ink, and (3) the date that particular ink formulation was first manufactured. Such requests should be made at least annually to be certain that your ink library is up to date. If you receive an ink standard from a company that is very similar to a standard you already have, ask the manufacturer how this standard differs from the similar ink standard.

Because not all ink companies are willing to spend the time to keep your ink library current, you will have to supplement the company obtained standards with standards (pens) you purchase in retail stores. When you do this, you should inquire of the pen company that makes the ink that is put into their pens. This is necessary to get the information referred to above. Many pen companies do not make their own inks, but they purchase the inks from large suppliers, such as National Ink or Dokumental. You should purchase all the different pens that are available and do this at least annually. It is a good idea to make purchases in different regions of the country, or even different countries, to make sure your ink library is as complete as possible. A comprehensive ink library will have several thousand ink standards.

It is strongly recommended that you take the time to visit as many different ink companies as possible. This will not only increase your knowledge of how inks are made, but it will help you to establish contacts with the various companies. Once they know you, they will be more willing to help you.

DOCUMENTING YOUR INK LIBRARY

You must keep a file on each different ink manufacturer. The file should contain all correspondence to and from the ink companies, as well as any specific information you learn regarding ingredients of the inks. You should record the date you received or purchased the ink, and the date the ink was first manufactured and/or discontinued.

STORING THE INK STANDARDS

The ink standards should be placed on plain white photocopy paper. If the standards consist of ink in pens, write a whole page of writing. If the standard consists of bulk liquid ink in a bottle or tube, then smear the ink onto the paper using a cotton swab. Again, fill a whole page with the ink. Allow the ink on paper to completely dry before storing the written ink standard in a file or notebook. It is important to minimize exposure of the inks to light to minimize fading of the ink. The ink standards should be stored according to (1) the type of ink and (2) the color of ink. This will facilitate retrieval of the proper ink standard when you want to compare a questioned ink with the standard ink.

TLC ANALYSIS OF INK STANDARDS

Every ink standard in your ink library must be analyzed by TLC and the plate must be stored for future use in the identification of questioned inks. You should analyze each ink using different concentrations on the same TLC plate, from very weak to heavy concentrations. Merck plastic-backed HPTLC plates are recommended because these plates are less susceptible to breaking when handled and stored. As above, the TLC plates should be stored according to the type and color of ink in envelopes of suitable size and away from light. Appropriate TLC procedures to be used have been previously described.

After all of your ink standards have been analyzed by TLC, you are ready to begin ink identifications. This statement assumes you have completed a comprehensive training program under the supervision of an experienced ink chemist.

Chapter 8

INK DATING

BACKGROUND

Age determination of ink dates back to the 1920s, when iron gallotannate inks were proven to have aging properties. Researchers found that the migration of chloride or sulfate ions along the fibers of paper was related to ink age. A complete discussion of early ink dating research is available in the *Forensic Examination of Ink and Paper*[1] and an excellent summary of ink dating research from past to present is described by Cantu in reference.[2]

THE AGING PROCESS

Inks contain several substances that can age with time. This aging may be as simple as evaporation of volatile substances or as complex as oxidation of certain ingredients and the hardening of ink resins on the surface of paper. Inks consist of colorants such as dyes and pigments, and a carrier solvent, called a *vehicle* by the ink industry. Resins and fatty acids, like oleic acid, are used as drying agents—and to adjust the viscosity of the ink. The solvents evaporate with time and the resins harden by oxidation or polymerization. Each of these aging properties causes measurable changes in the ink.[3] Two commonly measured aging properties are how well an ink extracts into a weak solvent and how much solvent (carrier) remains in the ink. Solvent evaporation and resin hardening contribute to the aging of fresh inks up to about one year old.

For inks that are over a year old, the hardening of resins is the main factor of aging. Because most documents are at least a year old by the time they are examined by an ink dating chemist, most research has been concentrated on methods that involve how well an ink extracts into weak solvents.

CURRENT STATUS OF INK DATING

The dating of inks on questioned documents has become routine in the United States, because of the great demand for these services during criminal investigations and civil litigations and because knowledge of these capabilities is now widespread throughout the world.

Since the development of the first techniques for dating inks on questioned documents in 1968, there have been many advances in this field. Further, these advances have passed the Frye and Daubert tests on many occasions and are therefore, routinely accepted in U.S. courts. Testimony using these advanced methods has also been accepted in Israel, Japan, Hong Kong, and Australia. It is safe to say that government and private ink dating chemists have testified approximately 1000 times using these methods.

FIRST DATE OF PRODUCTION METHOD

The inks in question are identified using the procedures described in Chapter 5. After you identify the ink, obtain and verify the first date of production of that specific formulation by the manufacturer of that ink formulation. If the manufacturer did not produce and market the ink until after the date that the document was purportedly prepared, then obviously the document could not have been written on that date. The questioned document (or entry) had to have been written some time after the ink was first commercially available–and then backdated.

INK TAG METHOD

Ink tags are chemicals that fluoresce under longwave ultraviolet light. If an ink tag is identified in an ink, it is possible to determine the actual year or years the ink was made. Starting about 1970, the ink manufacturer, Formulabs, began adding ink tags to some ballpoint inks; however, the use of these tags was discontinued in June, 1994.

Ink dating tags used by Formulabs can be detected and identified by TLC using a solvent system of chlorobenzene and ethyl acetate (5:1) respectively. Standard samples of the various tags must be run simultaneously on the same plate as the questioned inks. If present, the tags are viewed under longwave ultraviolet light and the R_f values of the tags present in the questioned inks are compared with the R_f values of the standard tags. Since Formulabs considered these tags proprietary information, we can provide no further information about the tags here. Formulabs should be contacted directly if this information is needed.

RELATIVE AGE COMPARISON METHODS

Dating inks by these procedures is based on the scientifically proven premise that as ink ages on paper, there are corresponding changes in the solubility properties of the ink. As described earlier, these changes correspond to solvent evaporation and the hardening of resins from oxidation and polymerization.[4] Therefore, by comparing the solubility or extraction properties of questioned inks with known dated inks of the same formulation, written on the same type of paper and stored under similar conditions, it becomes possible to estimate how long ago an ink entry was written on a document.

The methods used to measure the rate and extent of extraction of inks into weak solvents are called the R-Ratio (rate of extraction) and the Percent of Extraction (extent of extraction) methods.[5] Another method used is the Dye Ratio method, which measures the changes in solubility of the individual dyes in inks with age, as well as fading of some of the dyes, and degradation of certain dyes.[6] Recent research has shown that the effect of different paper and different storage conditions on relative ink age comparisons may be minimal. This research will be described in detail in Chapter 10.

The age of inks consisting of the same formulation can also be compared without known dated writings, to determine whether the writings were made at the same or different times. This is true only if the inks being compared are still aging (drying). After the ink has "aged out" (completely dried) using these procedures, no differences in solubility properties are expected, even if the inks were written at different times.[7] Typically, inks will become completely dry (as measured by these procedures) within five years for ballpoint inks and three years for non ballpoint inks.

When matching inks are compared without known dated writings, it is possible to determine the sequence in which the inks were written. This, again, requires knowing that the inks are still aging–and knowing how the inks age. For example, some inks extract faster and more completely in organic solvents as the inks age; whereas other inks extract more slowly and less completely as the ink ages.[8] To determine which way the ink ages, heat a sample of the ink at 100° C for 30 minutes. Then compare the rate and extent of extraction of this heated sample into an organic solvent to an unheated sample of the same ink. This will tell you if the heated (totally aged) sample extracted faster and more completely than the unheated sample or vice versa.

Rate and Extent of Extraction Methods

- Using the syringe and plunger, remove 10–15 plugs of ink and paper and place them into the 1 dram glass vials. Cap and label the vial with the sample number. Repeat for each sample to be analyzed.
- Set the timer to 10 minutes.
- Using the automatic 20 μL pipette, add 20 μL of a weak solvent to the vial containing the ink sample and start the timer immediately. (For almost all ballpoint inks, 1-butanol is a good weak solvent.)
- Stir by rotating the vial containing the ink and weak solvent 5 times, immediately after adding the weak solvent, and just before removing each aliquot for spotting.
- Spot 4 μL aliquots of dissolved ink in one continuous application on the HPTLC plate at 1/2, 1 1/2, 3, and 10-minute intervals, stirring before removal of each aliquot. Place these spots side-by-side at one end of the plate, approximately 1 cm apart. (It may be necessary to use tweezers to remove the pipettes from the glass vial.) Note: If a non-ballpoint ink is being analyzed, it may be necessary to spot the 4 μL aliquots intermittently to prevent the spot from getting too large. The spot should be no larger than 0.3 cm O.D.
- Repeat the above procedures for each sample to be analyzed.

- Evaporate the solvent remaining in the vials in an oven at 80° C for 15 minutes.
- Remove the vials from the oven and allow to cool to room temperature and equilibrate with temperature and humidity in the room. (This takes about one hour.)
- Using the automatic pipette, add 10 μL of a strong solvent to each vial and allow to extract for 15 minutes. (Benzyl alcohol is the solvent of choice for ballpoint inks and some non-ballpoint inks. Pyridine is satisfactory, but you must exercise care to keep the spots small, when spotting. Some non-ballpoint inks may require using ethanol and water (1:1) or DMSO for water resistant non-ballpoint inks.)
- Spot 4 μL of the ink extracted with the strong solvent, adjacent to the 10-minute weak solvent spot. (If benzyl alcohol was used as the strong solvent, spot in one continuous application of the pipette to the plate. If pyridine was used, spot intermittently to keep the spot from getting too large.)
- Repeat the above steps for each sample.
- Dry the spots on the plate in an oven at 80° C for about 15 minutes or until the white ring around the benzyl alcohol spot has disappeared.
- Remove the plate from the oven and allow to cool to room temperature.
- Scan the plate in the scanning TLC densitometer along the path of the 4 weak solvent spots and the one strong solvent spot and read the relative concentrations of the 5 spots.
- Repeat the scan described above for each sample.
- Calculate the various rates of extractions (R-Ratios) for each sample by letting the percent of ink extracted in the weak solvent at 10 minutes equal to one. Then calculate the R-Ratios for each time interval of 1/2, 1 1/2, 3, and 10 minutes. This provides a normalized, mass independent curve.
- To obtain R-Ratio curves, plot R-Ratios vs. time of extraction (see Fig. 8.1).

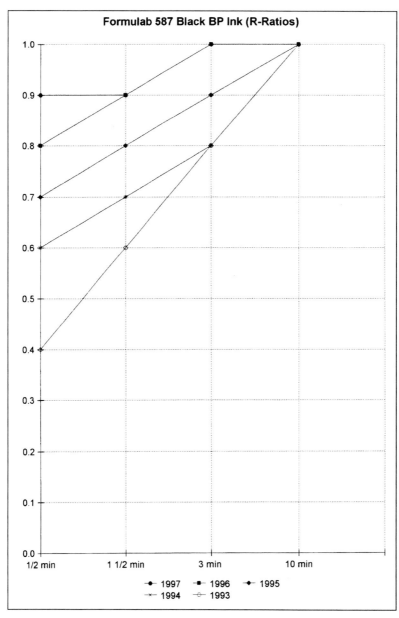

Figure 8.1. R-ratios.

Compare the R-Ratio curves of all inks tested of the same formulation. To estimate the age of the questioned inks, compare the R-Ratio curves of the questioned inks with the R-Ratio curves of the known dated inks.

Extent or Percent Extraction Calculations

Calculate the percent or extent of ink extracted in the weak solvent at the various time intervals by dividing the densitometer reading for each weak solvent spot by the total amount of ink extracted in the weak and strong solvent, then multiply by 100 (see Fig. 8.2).

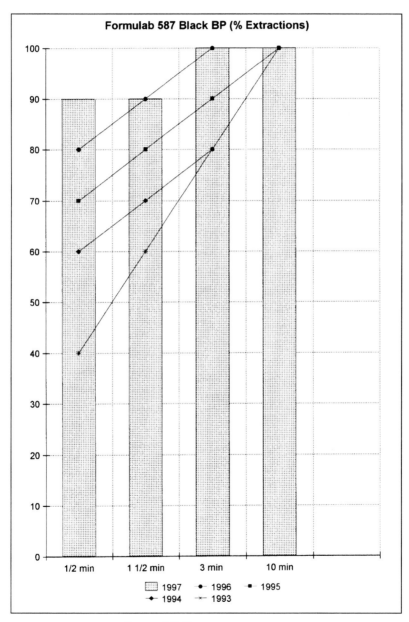

Figure 8.2. Percent extractions.

Note: You can perform a simplified percent extraction procedure by extracting each sample for just one minute in the weak solvent; then after spotting this one-minute extract, add the strong solvent directly to the weak solvent extract remaining in the vial. After allowing the strong solvent to extract for 15 minutes, spot the strong solvent extract right beside the one-minute weak solvent extraction spot. This procedure produces just two spots to measure in the densitometer.

While this procedure eliminates R-Ratio determinations, it improves the accuracy, sensitivity, and reproducibility of the percent extraction measurements by reducing the number of steps in the procedure. If this simplified procedure is followed, only 10 μL of weak solvent is needed and sample size can be reduced to five or fewer plugs of ink.[9]

Dye Ratio Measurements

Dye ratio measurements are based on several factors.[10] Researchers have established that the relative concentrations of dyes in inks change as the ink ages on paper, but the concentrations of the dyes do not always change at the same rate. Therefore, by measuring dye ratios in inks (the ratio of the amount of one dye with respect to the amounts of other dyes present), it becomes possible to date questioned inks—when known dated writings of the same ink are available for comparison. The changes that occur in the relative concentrations of the dyes are not limited to changes in the solubility characteristics of the inks.

Other changes in the inks over time that affect dye ratios are fading of the various dyes in the inks and degradation or decomposition of the dyes present. For example, methyl violet, a common purple dye used in ballpoint inks, in its purest form is seen as a single dye by TLC. However, as the ink ages, methyl violet often can have as many as four bands by TLC.

Because changes in dye ratios are attributed to several factors, you may sometimes find it necessary to compare dye ratios in inks using two steps. If fading is the major factor in the aging of the ink, use a strong solvent, such as pyridine to completely extract all of the dyes present in the ink. Then measure the dyes separated on the HPTLC plate using a scanning TLC densitometer. However, when changes in solubility of the dyes in the ink is the main factor of aging, use a weak solvent, such a 1-butanol as the extracting solvent. This is the most common procedure.

The dye ratio method described below is part of a multiple sequential approach, which performs all three methods (R-Ratio, Percent of Extraction and Dye Ratio) on the same HPTLC plate. This approach works well with most inks and it provides the maximum amount of information in the least amount of time.[11] However, as previously described, for some inks in which fading or degradation is involved, you may find it necessary to run the dye ratio test separately. The procedure is as follows:

- Develop the HPTLC plate containing all the spots from the R-Ratio and Percent Extraction measurements in a solvent system of ethyl acetate, ethanol and water (70:35:30) respectively for 15 minutes.
- Dry the plate in an oven at 80° C for 10 minutes; then allow the plate to cool to room temperature.
- Scan each sample in the scanning densitometer along the direction of the dyes separated in each sample. From the densitometer readings, calculate all possible dye ratios for each sample.
- For example, divide dye 3 by dye 1, divide dye 3 by dye 2 and divide dye 2 by dye 1. Compare the dye ratios obtained for questioned and known dated inks to estimate the age of the questioned inks (see Fig. 8.3).

Inks with matching dye ratios are consistent with having been written at the same time. If inks exhibit dye ratios that do not match, this generally means that the inks were written at different times, unless one ink had an unusually large batch variation. If inks allegedly written over a time span of several years are found to have the same dye ratios, it means these writings were all written at the same time, because the dye ratios would have changed over time if the writings were made contemporaneously.

Age Discriminating Power of the R-Ratio, Percent Extraction and Dye Ratio Methods

It is important to know that, depending on the ink formulation being tested and the paper on which the ink is written, each of the above methods may not all have equal ability to discriminate the age of the inks being analyzed. For example, it is not uncommon for one

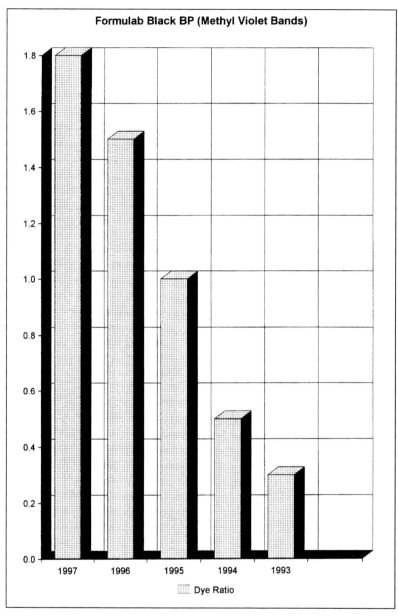

Figure 8.3. Dye ratios.

method to detect differences in age, when one or both of the other methods fail to detect these differences. This fact does not negate the results of the one method that did detect differences in age. The results are only negated when the results of one test conflict with the results of another test.

ACCELERATED AGING

The concept of accelerated aging (artificial aging) as a method for estimating the age of paper is well established.[12] Heat has been used to artificially age paper and changes in the folding endurance of the paper are measured. Cantu seized upon this approach for estimating the age of inks by accelerated aging (heating).[13] He established an equivalence between natural and induced aging of a Fisher black ballpoint ink written on Nashua photocopy paper. The aging parameter he used was the extent of extraction into a weak solvent of a fluorescent Rhodoamine type dye present in this ink. He made fluorescent measurements on the extracts. For this ink, paper and aging parameter, four minutes of induced aging at 100° C was equivalent to 72 days of natural aging at room temperature (22° C). This work established the feasibility of accelerated aging as an alternative method of estimating the age of inks, even when no known dated inks are available for comparison with questioned inks.

Brunelle[14,15] and Brunelle and Speckin[16] took Cantu's work further and applied the accelerated aging technique to actual casework. Presently, the accelerated aging technique for estimating the age of inks is routinely accepted by the courts. It is endorsed by the Society of Forensic Ink Analysts and is used by all qualified ink dating chemists in the private sector.

In situations where known dated writings are not available for comparison with questioned inks, you can perform accelerated aging of a questioned sample to estimate its age. Heat the questioned ink sample at 100° C for 30 minutes to totally age (totally dry out) the ink sample. This process creates or mimics a standard ink that is several years old, depending on how long it takes for the particular ink formulation in question to totally dry out. By comparing the relative age of the heated ink sample with an unheated sample of the same ink, you can determine if the questioned ink is still in the aging or drying process (using any of the previously described ink dryness tests).

For example, if the ink in question is a Bic black ballpoint ink and there were no changes caused by heating this ink, then you can conclude that the writing is three or more years old, because researchers have established that this Bic ink stops aging after three years, using the techniques described in this book.

Conversely, if the heating caused significant changes in R-ratios, dye ratios or percents of extraction, then you can be conclude that this ink is still drying and is less than three years old. The greater the change caused by heat, the newer the ink is. Heating the ink causes smaller and smaller changes as the ink approaches total dryness. For this reason, you can reach conclusions as to whether the ink is approaching total dryness or whether the ink was written quite recently.

Procedure

Accelerated aging involves just one additional step before the R-ratio, dye ratio, or percent extraction measurements are made.

Remove duplicate samples of the ink to be examined, one for heating and the other to test without heating. Heat the heated sample for 30 minutes at $100°$ C. Allow it to cool and equilibrate with the temperature and humidity in the room for one hour. Then analyze the heated and unheated samples using the ink dryness tests described earlier.

DETERMINATION OF INK AGE DIFFERENCES BY STATISTICAL ANALYSIS OF DENSITOMETRIC DATA

In Chapter 5, we briefly covered statistical analysis for analytical chemistry. In Chapter 8, we have examined use of densitometric measurements of TLC for ink age determination.

The densitometric data, which form the aging curves, provides evidence of ink age differences through graphical relationship of the distribution of individual measurements. Artificial aging reveals the direction of the aging parameters if the direction is not already known from past experience with the ink. Each point on the aging curve is a mean value of densitometric measurements performed on spots or thin layer chromatograms. Standard deviations from these means are called "error bars" or "confidence limits."

Over the past few years, ink analysts have conducted studies of the relationship between age of inks and confidence limits calculated from duplicate and triplicate measurements of ink samples. At a Board meeting of the Society of Forensic Ink Analysts in August 1999, members came to a unanimous decision regarding the threshold for a statistically significant difference between two samples. That threshold was established as "one standard deviation." This is based on the error

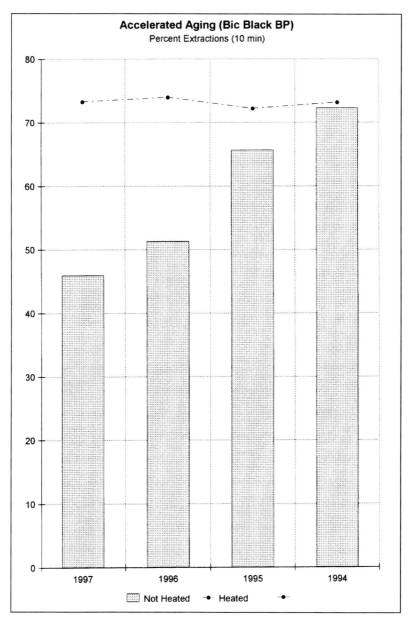

Figure 8.4. Accelerated aging.

in measurements of duplicate or triplicate samples, when compared to the arithmetic mean of the sample group. This means that, if values on compared aging curves each lie outside one standard deviation of each other, the ink samples represented by the aging curves are demonstrated to be of different ages. This threshold value has been testified to and accepted in courts since this meeting.

REFERENCES

1. Brunelle, R. L. & Reed, R. W.: *Forensic Examination of Ink and Paper*. Springfield, IL: Charles C Thomas, 1984.
2. Cantu, A. A.: A sketch of analytical methods for document dating part II. The dynamic approach: Determining age dependent analytical profiles. *Int. J. Forensic Document Examiners*, 2: 192, 1996.
3. Ibid
4. Ibid.
5. Cantu, A. A. & Prough, R. S.: On the relative aging of inks–the solvent extraction technique. *JFS*, 32: 1151, 1987.
6. Brunelle, R. L. & Lee, H.: Determining the relative age of ball-point ink using a single-solvent extraction mass independent approach. *JFS*, 34: 1166, 1989.
7. Brunelle, R. L. & Speckin, E. J.: Technical report with case studies on the accelerated aging of ball-point inks. *Int. J. Forensic Document Examiners*, 4: 240, 1998.
8. Ibid.
9. Brunelle, R. L.: A sequential multiple approach to determining the relative age of writing inks. *Int. J. Forensic Document Examiners*, 1: 94, 1995.
10. See 6 above.
11. See 9 above.
12. Priest, D. J.: Artificial aging of paper: Correlation with natural aging. Proceedings on the effects of aging on printing and writing papers. ASTM Institute for Standards Research, *ASTM*, Philadelphia, 1994.
13. Cantu, A. A.: Comments on the accelerated aging of inks. *JFS*, 33: 744, 1998.
14. Brunelle, R. L.: Ink dating–the state of the art. *JFS*, 37: 113, 1992.
15. See 9 above.
16. See 7 above.

Chapter 9

OTHER METHODS FOR DATING WRITING INKS

SCANNING AUGER MICROSCOPY

While relative age (ink dryness) comparisons are by far the most extensively used tests for dating inks, researchers have developed additional methods. In 1984, McNeil reported the use of scanning Auger microscopy for dating manuscript iron gallotannate inks.[1,2]

Scanning Auger microscopy (SAM) involves focusing an electron beam on a sample and measuring emitted "Auger electrons," which identify elements present by their discrete energy levels. SAM can measure a 3–5 nm depth[3] with a spatial resolution of about 5 nm.

Used for ink dating, this procedure measures the outward migration of iron atoms from the ink boundary along the fibers in the paper. The migration increases exponentially with the age of iron gallotannate ink. Researchers have reported that the iron migrates about one micron every 29 years and continues for over 700 years. Absolute dating of this class of ink is possible, because this procedure is not affected by temperature or humidity. Scanning Auger microscopy is limited to historical documents, because the accuracy is limited to plus or minus about 22 years. Nevertheless this technique is useful for dating iron gallotannate inks on old documents, such as the case involving the "Salamander Letter." McNeil also used his procedure on the Mark Hoffman forgeries in Utah, the Jack the Ripper diary, the "Oath of a Freeman,[4]" and the alleged sixth draft of the Gettysburg Address.

Theory

Equipped with a special primary electron source cathode, the instrument focuses an electron beam on the sample and bombards the sample with electrons. This process causes the ejection of Auger electrons from each atom above atomic number 15 in the sample. The energy of the ejected electrons is dependent on the atomic number of the atom. The escape depth of these electrons is 10 Angstroms. This makes the SAM a highly specific surface analysis technique.

Procedure

Use an eight-gauge hollow hypodermic needle to remove samples of the ink and paper from five different locations on the document. Make triplicate measurements at each site (same fibril).

McNeil takes measurements perpendicular to the ink line and the iron count grows sharply as the sample probe enters the ink area and decreases sharply as the probe leaves the ink area. To obtain mass independence, he normalizes curves to 100%. All iron count vs. distance curves begin at 100% and drop down to an inflection at about 4.7 μm from the ink edge. This portion of the curve is called the "lead tail" and is the same for all inks. After this, the curves descend in an exponen-

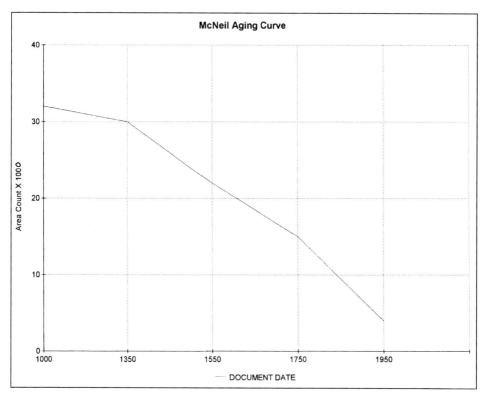

Figure 9.1. McNeil curve.

tial manner to zero–at a distance that is characteristic of the ink age. As the age of the ink increases, the shape of the tail becomes less steep and it levels off to zero at a progressively longer distance (see Fig. 9.1).

FOURIER TRANSFORM INFRARED SPECTROSCOPY

Howard Humecki from McCrone Associates in Chicago developed a totally different approach to dating inks. His method is based on the measurement of the -OH band at 3 microns, the -CH band at 3.4 microns and the -CO band at 5.8 microns–in a blue ballpoint ink made by Formulabs (their formula 353). He found IR spectra of these bands change with age, suggesting that both evaporation of volatile components and oxidation occurred in the ballpoint ink as it aged. The mass invariant ratio of the -OH band and the -CH band decreased monotonically with age and this decrease leveled off after about 20 years.[5] For some reason, this method for dating inks has not been widely utilized in the forensic examination and dating of inks, since it was developed by Humecki. However, this method still shows great promise and deserves further study.

Method

He removed ink samples from the document (1/4 inch samples), then extracted with pyridine and transferred the ink extract to a salt window. He used a 1 x 4 mm masking window with a 6x beam condenser on a Digilab FRS-20 infrared spectrometer with a triglycine sulfate cell window.

Humecki ran spectra for ink samples ranging from 1 to 20 years in age. Controls for salt and for paper showed very little interference from the paper extract or the triglycine sulfate. He also developed a method for the microanalysis of 1mm microdiscs of ink sample.

FTIR Dating of Artificially Aged Bulk Ballpoint Pen Ink

Jian Wang, of Tsinghua University, Beijing, et al. (cited in Chapter 6 for FTIR differentiation of ballpoint inks) used heating and ultraviolet irradiation to artificially age blue ballpoint ink samples.[6] Both methods demonstrated a change in FTIR peak height ratios between 1000 and 1600 cm^{-1}. Thus, at least in these blue ballpoint pen inks, artificial age changes produce demonstrable changes in FTIR spectra.

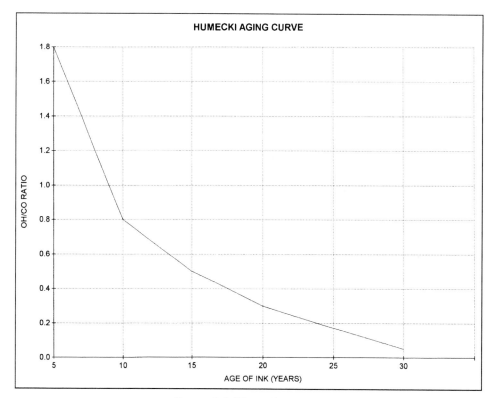

Figure 9.2. Humecki curve.

MASS SPECTROMETRY, GAS CHROMATOGRAPHY AND GC-MS

Measurement of Volatile Components by GC-MS

Valerie Aginsky of Moscow, Russia (now living in the United States), has been a prolific publisher of papers using GC-MS to date inks. His methods primarily involve measurement of the changes in the volatile components in inks with age.[7] He does this by comparison with known dated inks and by accelerated aging, which he calls "absolute aging." GC-MS shows great promise for strengthening ink identifications, because it can be used to identify both volatile and non-volatile ingredients of ink. The technique also shows promise for dating inks less than six months old–by measuring the disappearance of the vehicle of the ink. The vehicle is the solvent in which all other ink ingredients are either dissolved or dispersed. GC alone can also do this. However, at this point, this method of Aginsky cannot be used to date inks on documents over six months old. Since most documents encountered during investigations are much older than six months, his methods are of limited value. It is also important to mention that researchers in the United States have not been able to reproduce Aginsky's techniques, primarily because Aginsky's published works do not contain all the parameters needed to apply his techniques.

Methods

Although all the needed parameters are not available to apply these methods, the following descriptions provide the general approach for these techniques.

VEHICLE-TO-DYE RATIO. First, extract a 2 cm sample of ink with carbon tetrachloride for 60 minutes and run the ink extract on a GC. Using an internal standard in the carbon tetrachloride, measure the concentrations of volatile components present in two ways. First calculate the ratio of volatile components. Next, extract, evaporate, and dry the remainder. Extract the residue again with 1.2 mL dimethylformamide to remove the dyes, and then run a UV-Visible spectrum on this extract to obtain the wavelength of maximum absorption. Next, calculate the ratio of the vehicle content to absorbance value at the absorbance maximum. The ratios level off at about 70 days for the Italian, violet ballpoint ink tested.

RATIO OF SEQUENTIAL SOLVENT EXTRACTIONS. This method is similar to the Extent-of-Extraction method described in Chapter 8, except that you use different extraction solvents–and GC is the measurement tool in lieu of TLC followed by TLC Densitometry. Volatile components are measured instead of non-volatile dye components. First extract the ink into a weak solvent (carbon tetrachloride) for one hour and run a GC.

Then remove the remaining solvent and dry the sample. Next, add chloroform as the strong solvent and allow to extract for two minutes, and run a GC on this extract. Calculate the percent of volatile component as:

$$\% \text{ Volatile Component} = \frac{\text{Conc. in weak solvent X 100}}{\text{Conc. in weak solvent} + \text{Conc. in strong solvent}}$$

Again, the amount of volatile component levels off after the ink is about 3 months old for the same Italian, blue-violet ballpoint ink.

Accelerated Aging

Take two portions of the same ink entry. Heat one portion and do not heat the other. Then perform the weak and strong solvent extractions as described above and measure the differences in the levels of volatile components by GC-MS. Heat the one sample for one hour at 70° C, instead of 100° C as described in Chapter 8. For accelerated aging tests, the weak solvent is a mixture of carbon tetrachloride and chloroform. The relative concentration of each is unknown. Use a 30-minute weak solvent extraction time with an internal standard, followed by a two-minute extraction in chloroform. The differences in the percent extractions of the heated and unheated ink samples level off between six and 12 months, depending on the ink and the volatile component extracted.

You can use a procedure similar to the above with different extracting solvents. For example, you can extract the ink with acetonitrile containing m-cresol as an internal standard. GC-MS can identify benzyl alcohol, phenoxyethanol (common vehicles in ballpoint inks), and phthalic anhydride (a solid volatile component). 2-pyrrolidone can be found in jet printer ink. Diethylene glycol can be found in ballpoint, stamp pad, roller ball, and porous tip pen inks. No differences in the amount of volatile components can be seen after the ink is about six months old.

Solid Phase Micro-Extraction Mass Spectrometry

This technique, described by Luc Brazeau, Mohinder Chauhan, and Marc Gaudreau,[8] requires a specially constructed, fused silica fiber coated with a polymeric phase mounted in a syringe. The sampling end of the fiber is placed against the written ink line. Volatile analytes from the ink are adsorbed into the capillary until an equilibrium is reached in the system.

The analyte is then desorbed through mass spectrometry using a mass selective detector. The mass spectra are analyzed for the ink volatiles, the relative abundance of which is related to the age of the ink.

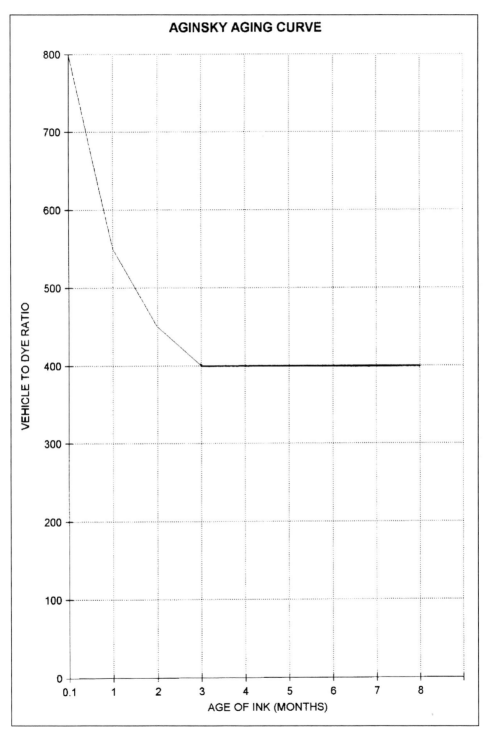

Figure 9.3. Aginsky curve.

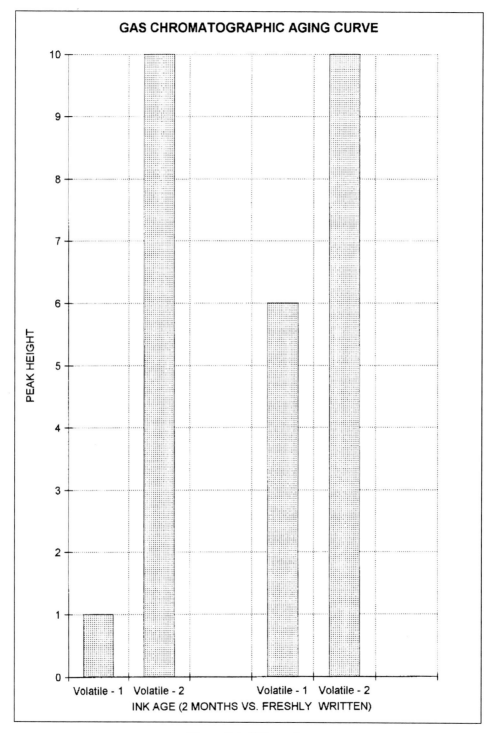

Figure 9.4. GC graph.

Laser Desorption/Ionization Mass Spectrometry

LD-MS uses a pulsed laser to desorb molecular species from a sample for MS detection.

Donna Grim, John Allison, and Jay Alan Siegel reported in 2001 use of LD-MS to date ink-jet printer and ballpoint pen inks.[9] They artificially aged inks using UV irradiation (254 nm. 760 microwatts/sq. cm) in one-hour increments to 12 hours.

- Instrumentation: PE Biosystems MALDI using modified plate bearing sample paper with ink.
- Degradation products formed by oxidative demethylation of methyl violet 2B were detected in ink artificially aged 12 hours.
- Age of the ink is established by comparison of ratios of such degradation products to initial base peak.

LDMS can analyze inks directly on paper. If the spectrometer's sample plate is modified to accept the entire document bearing the questioned ink, the procedure is essentially non-destructive.

Time-of-Flight Secondary Ion Mass Spectrometry (TOF-SIMS)

TOF-SIMS bombards a sample surface with an ion beam to remove atoms from the outermost atomic layer of the surface. Primary ions striking the surface cause extraction of secondary ions that are directed into a time-of-flight mass spectrometer.

The velocities of the secondary ions are proportional to their mass/charge ratios (m/z), thus the secondary ions are dispersed in time according to their velocities, with ions of differing mass detected as a function of time.

Albert Lyter and P.J. McKeown presented a study in 2001 of ballpoint ink samples written in 1993, 1994, and 2000. Using TOF-SIMS, these researchers reported distinguishing the above samples by detection of different proportions of ions characteristic of each ink age.[10]

As other analysts test these techniques, scientific organizations such as SOFIA will report the usefulness and reliability of the techniques.

HIGH-PERFORMANCE LIQUID CHROMATOGRAPHY

HPLC is not widely used for dating inks, but it is mentioned in this chapter because it has the potential to be of value in this area. The extraction methods require great manipulative skills by the examiner and the method is mass dependent, meaning equal amounts of ink must be compared.

In 2002, Andrasko used HPLC with a diode array detector (190 nm–600 nm) to investigate decomposition of ink on a document stored in darkness.[11] Blue ballpoint pens containing ink of the same composition were used. Entries included fresh ink, ink at nine months, and then at four-month intervals through approximately two years. Spectra of the entries demonstrated progressive demethylation of the ink dyes Methyl Violet, Crystal Violet, and Tetramethyl Para Rosalinine. (Compare this procedure to that of Allison and Siegel, above.)

Daylight increased dye decomposition 30-fold over storage in darkness. Therefore, if parts of a document were exposed to different amounts of light over time, this could complicate interpretation of such analyses. Decomposition was also affected by heat, ink thickness, and paper composition.

Issacs and Clayton[12] reported a procedure they applied to seven ballpoint inks. They extracted a single ink plug continuously using a polar solvent into an HPLC micro flow cell with a diode array spectrophotometer. They plotted absorbance at a specific wavelength vs. time of extraction. The graph began with a sharp rise from zero as the extraction began, but then the graph returns back to zero as the extraction ends. The only mass invariant measurement available with this method is a measure of the rate of extraction, but even this proved unreliable.

ALTERNATIVE METHODS FOR
ACCELERATED AGING OF INKS

The procedures described in this book for accelerated aging of inks have been tested extensively and accepted in the courts. These procedures use heat treatment of the sample to artificially age the ink. In Chapter 8, we examined how heat treatment is used to determine which way the ink ages with respect to extraction rate. Therefore, heat treatment will likely continue to be suitable for this purpose. However, recent research has indicated irradiation of ink by shortwave UV can also be used for this purpose. John Allison and Donna Grim[13] pointed out in 2001 that shortwave UV irradiation may be a better method for accelerated aging of inks, if the subsequent analysis is directed toward detection of reaction products of solvent and dye molecules. Unlike heat, UV irradiation does not cause rapid evaporation of solvents in the ink. It permits examination of such dye degradation products.

REFERENCES

1. McNeil, R. J.: Scanning Auger microscopy for dating manuscript inks. *Archeological Chemistry III*, J.B. Lambert, Ed., Advances in Chemistry Series, No. 205, *ACS*, Washington, 255, 1984.
2. McNeil, R. J.: Scanning Auger microscopy for manuscript dating. *Literary Research, 13*: 137, 1988.
3. Surface Science Western, Room G1, Western Science Centre, The University of Western Ontario, London, ON N6A 5B7 (Website).
4. McNeil, R. J.: Scanning Auger microscopy for dating two copies of the "Oath of Freeman"–the judgment of the experts: Essays and documents about the investigation of the forging of the Oath of a Freeman, J. Gilbreath, Ed., *American Antiquarian Society*, Worcester, 115, 1991.
5. Humecki, H.: Experiments in ballpoint ink aging using infrared spectroscopy. Proceedings of the International Symposium on Questioned Documents, 1985, FBI Academy, Quantico, VA. U.S. Government Printing Office, Washington, pp 131–135.
6. Wang, J, Luo, G., Sun, S. & Wang, Y.: Systematic analysis of bulk blue ballpoint pen ink by FTIR spectrometry. JFS 2001; 46(5):1093–1097.
7. Aginsky, V. N.: Dating and characterizing writing, stamp pad and jet printer inks by gas chromatography/mass spectrometry. *Int. J. Forensic Document Examiners*, 2: 103, 1996.
8. Brazeau, L., Chauhan, M. & Gaudreau, M.: The use of micro-extraction in the development of a method to determine the ageing characteristics of inks. Presented at the 2000 Meeting of the American Society of Questioned Document Examiners.
9. Grim, D. M., Allison, J. & Seigel, J. A.: Determining the age of ink on a questioned document using laser desorption/ionization mass spectrometry. Presented at the 2001 Meeting of the American Academy of Forensic Sciences.
10. Lyter, A. H. III & Windsor, P. J.: A study of time-of-flight secondary ion mass spectrometry (TOF-SIMS) as a tool for the dating of writing ink. Presented at the 2001 Meeting of the American Academy of Forensic Sciences.
11. Andrasko, J.: Changes in composition of ballpoint pen inks on aging in darkness. *JFS* 2001; 47(2):324–327.
12. Isaacs, M. D. J. & Clayton, N. J : The examination of aged ball-point ink writing by solvent extraction/spectrophotometry. Technical Note No. 749, Central Research and Support Establishment, Home Office Forensic Science Service, Aldermasten, UK, 1990.

13. Allison, J. & Grim, D.: Is there a general method for the accelerated aging of ink on paper? Presented at the 2001 Meeting of the American Academy of Forensic Sciences.

Chapter 10

EXPERIMENTS REGARDING THE EFFECTS OF INK THICKNESS, PAPER, STORAGE CONDITIONS, LINEARITY OF DENSITOMETER MEASUREMENTS, AND THE AGING OF PAPER ON INK DRYNESS TESTS

INTRODUCTION

Some have raised concerns that the results of relative ink age (ink dryness tests) determinations may not be reliable because of several factors.[1] These factors include: ink thickness, paper, storage conditions, linearity of densitometer measurements, and the age of the paper on which the ink is written. This chapter reports the results of research performed by several members of the Society of Forensic Ink Analysts (SOFIA). This research answers these questions and confirms the reliability of all of the relative age comparison tests described in Chapter 7–the R-ratio, percent extraction and dye ratio methods.

INK THICKNESS TESTS

For this experiment, researchers used a Bic black ballpoint pen writing with pen pressure from light to heavy on plain white copy paper. Four private ink-dating chemists examined the ink samples in duplicate using the simplified percent extraction procedure (measuring the percent of ink extracted in 1-butanol at one minute extraction time). The results of these tests confirm that there are no significant effects of ink thickness on this percent extraction measurement of the amount of ink extracted in one minute. The results of this experiment are tabulated in Figure 10.1.

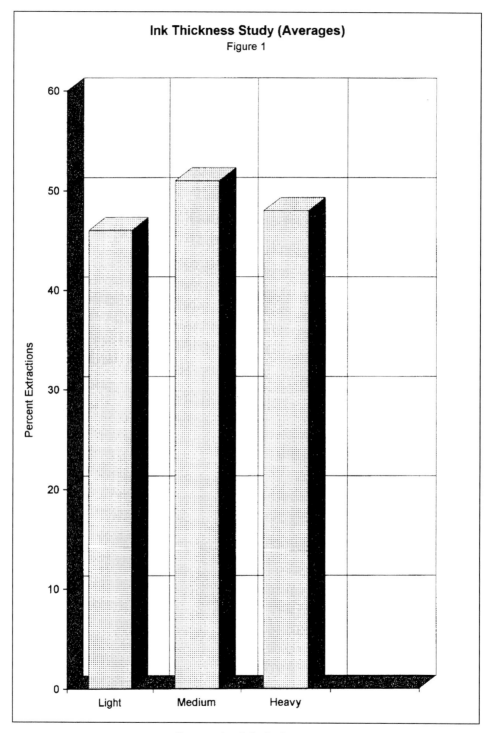

Figure 10.1. Ink thickness.

STORAGE CONDITIONS

For this study a Formulabs 587 black ballpoint ink was written on seven separate pages of plain white photocopier paper. The writings were stored from 1995 to 1998 in North Carolina, Florida, Pennsylvania, Arizona, Colorado, Oklahoma, and Alaska. These locations provided a wide range of climates from the very humid to the very dry and from the very cold to the very hot. All documents were stored under normal room temperature condition (storage buildings were heated in the winter and air-conditioned in the summer). The inks stored at the various locations were analyzed in duplicate by the simplified percent extraction procedure. The results of these tests confirm no significant effects on the aging of the inks stored under this wide range of climate conditions. This means that as long as documents are stored under normal room temperature conditions, different climates have no effect on the aging of the ink. The results of this experiment are shown in Figure 10.2.

LINEARITY OF TLC DENSITOMETRY MEASUREMENTS

To test the linearity of the densitometer measurements, researchers diluted a stock solution of a Bic black ballpoint ink with 1-butanol to 1/2, 1/4, 1/8, 1/16, and 1/32 of full strength. They then spotted each dilution of ink on a HPTLC plate. They allowed these to dry, and then scanned them in a Shimadzu, Model 930, Dual wavelength TLC Scanner.

A plot of the results of this experiment clearly demonstrates the line goes through zero and the measurements are indeed linear. Figure 10.3 shows the results of this experiment.

EFFECTS OF PAPER

In 1998, in North Carolina and Virginia, researchers used Bic black ballpoint ink to write on yellow lined, plain white photocopier, and white bond paper. They then examined the inks in duplicate using the simplified percent extraction procedure. Figure 10.4 shows that the ink age determinations were not significantly different, even though the inks were written on different types of paper and in two different locations. This means that paper has little to no effect on relative age comparison tests.

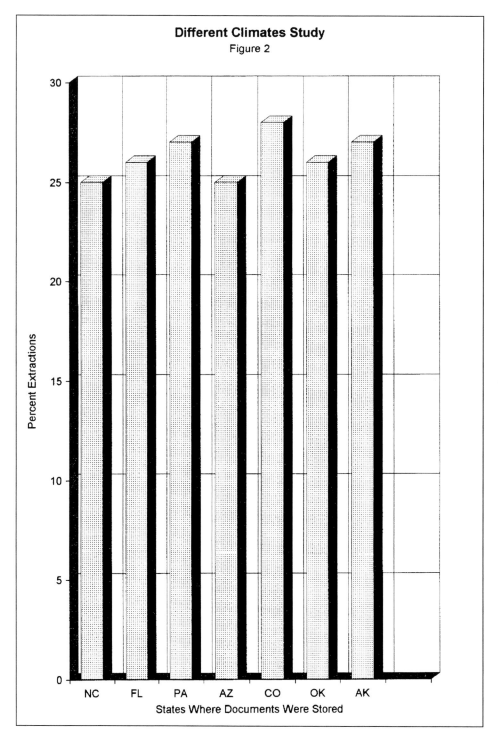

Figure 10.2. Storage conditions.

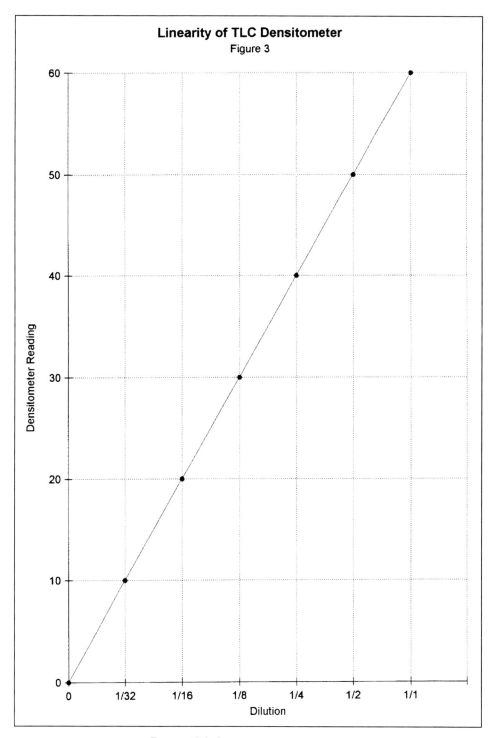

Figure 10.3. Linearity measurements.

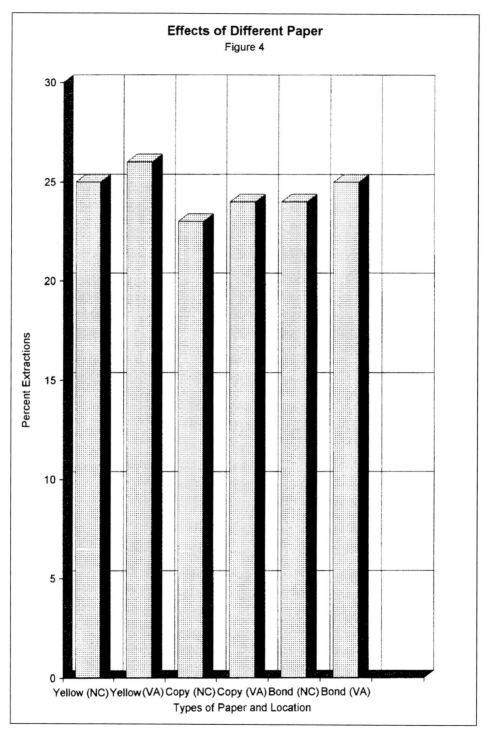

Figure 10.4. Effects of paper.

EFFECTS OF AGING OF PAPER ON
INK AGE DETERMINATIONS

Another question raised by some is, "What is the effect of the aging of paper on relative age comparison tests on inks?" Paper ages very slowly–as measured by its folding endurance. For example, at room temperature, it takes 19 years just to get to 1/2 way down the aging curve, another 19 years to get to 3/4 of the way down, and 19 more years to get to 7/8 of the way down the natural aging curve of paper. In fact it takes over 100 years to get to the point where no changes can be detected.[2]

In comparison to paper, inks written on paper age very fast. Natural aging curves for inks level off at six years or less–as measured by the R-ratio, percent extraction, and dye ratio methods.

Therefore there can be no detectable effect of the aging of paper on ink aging tests using these methods.

EFFECTS OF INK BATCH VARIATIONS

While ink manufacturers do try to control the addition of ingredients to inks within certain close tolerances, batch differences are occasionally inevitable for the following reasons:
1. The ink company is more interested in consistent color and viscosity of their ink than they are in adding precisely the same proportion of ingredients.
2. Ink companies don't throw ink away. Therefore, sometimes some left over ink gets combined into a new batch of either the same or even different ink formulations,
3. Some dyes purchased by ink companies, such as Methyl Violet, are not consistent in their quality. Sometimes this dye arrives to the ink manufacturer in its purest form as Crystal Violet; whereas, other times the Methyl Violet consists of several different isomers of Crystal Violet.
4. Contamination may occur from different ink formulations made in the same tank.
5. There is human error in measurement of ingredients.

These potential batch variations are the exception, rather than the rule. Nevertheless, these possible variations must be considered, when age comparisons are made using the dye ratio method. Figure 10.5 illustrates both consistent and inconsistent quality control during the manufacture of ink.

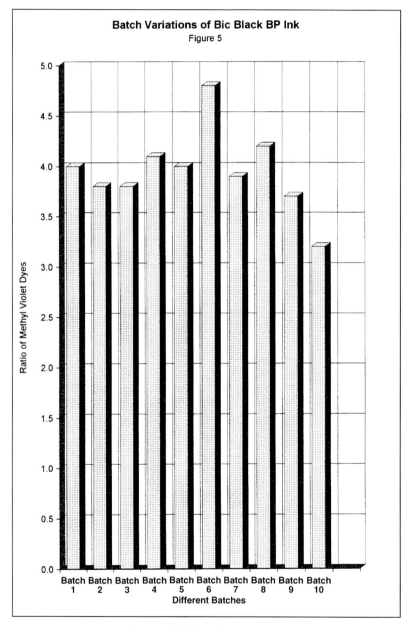

Figure 10.5. Batch variations.

Based on the studies reported in this chapter, it appears that the effects of storage conditions, as well as paper and ink thickness are minimal and have no significant effects on relative age comparison tests. To avoid potential error, examiners should still avoid ink age comparisons when they know that there are gross differences in the types of paper, ink thickness, and storage conditions. In addition, dye ratio comparisons for age determinations should be limited to those situations in which it is known that batch variations in the inks compared are not a significant factor. On the other hand, dye ratio comparisons are useful for determining whether two or more writings consist of the same or different batches of the same ink formulation.

REFERENCES

1. Aginsky, V.: Measuring ink extractability as a function of age–why the relative aging approach is unreliable and why it is more correct to measure ink volatile components than dyes. *Int. J. Forensic Document Examiners*, 4: 214, 1998.
2. Cantu, A. A.: A sketch of analytical methods for document dating part II. The dynamic approach: Determining age dependent analytical profiles. *Int. J. Forensic Document Examiners*, 2: 192, 1996.

Chapter 11

RESULTS OF ACTUAL CASE EXAMINATIONS USING R-RATIO, PERCENT EXTRACTION, AND DYE RATIO METHODS

Federal and private ink dating chemists in the United States have used these methods routinely since 1988. The author[1] has examined over 500 cases using these techniques during that time period and has testified to the results obtained, either at trials or depositions about 200 times.

The purpose of this chapter is to give the reader some actual examples of how these relative age comparison tests (ink dryness tests) were used to detect fraudulent documents or to show results consistent with authenticity of documents.

The six cases selected are intended to show the broad application of these ink dryness tests to a wide variety of investigations.

CASE 1

Case 1 involves an alleged medical malpractice case in which a physician was accused of negligence and malpractice. The patient was suffering from erectile dysfunction long before Pfizer developed Viagra®. One issue was whether the physician warned the patient that a particular surgery to correct this problem might substantially reduce the size of the patient's penis. The patient's medical record showed a detailed drawing of the surgery that was conducted and how this surgery might cause the reduction in size of the penis. The question was whether the drawing was made in the record in the presence of the patient in 1990–or was the drawing made after the lawsuit was filed in 1992.

The author analyzed the ink used for the drawing and found it to be a Formulabs black ballpoint ink containing a dating tag that proved this ink was manufactured in 1988.

Therefore this ink was available on the date of the document in 1990. In this case the only analyses that might still be useful to detect backdating of the drawing were the relative age comparison tests. Examination of other entries in the medical record determined that the same Formulab black ballpoint ink containing the same 1988 dating tag had been used over the time period of 1988 through 1991. This allowed for a direct comparison of the dryness of the ink in question with the known dated (unquestioned) inks in the record. All pages of the medical record consisted of plain white copy paper.

In this case, the author used all three methods (R-ratio, percent extraction, and dye ratio) for the relative age comparisons, as described in Chapter 8. Figure 11.1 shows the results of these examinations using the percent extraction procedure. Inspection of Figure 11.1 shows that the relative dryness of the questioned ink used for the drawing was higher than the same ink known to have been written in 1991 and much higher than the entry known to have been written in 1990. This proves the drawing had to have been written sometime after 1991 and could not have been written in 1990.

Comparison of the R-ratio curves for the same inks examined above revealed the questioned ink was extracting faster than the known 1991 ink and much faster than the known 1990 ink (see Figure 11.2). These results confirmed the results obtained using the percent extraction method.

Dye ratio measurements for the same inks described above showed a gradual and consistent change in the dye ratios from 1988 to 1991– with the dye ratios of the questioned ink being similar to the 1991 ink and dissimilar to the 1990 ink (see Figure 11.3).

Faced with this overwhelming evidence that the drawing in question was written after 1991 and not in 1990, the physician admitted the backdating of this entry in the medical record. The insurance carrier settled the case out of court.

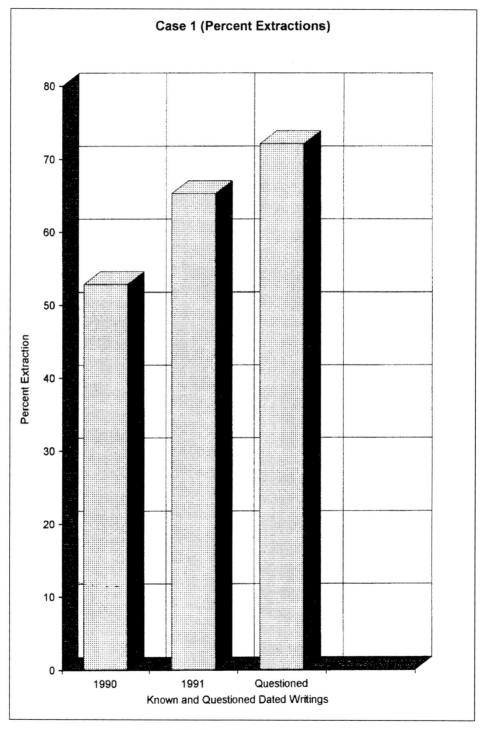

Figure 11.1. Case 1: Percent extractions.

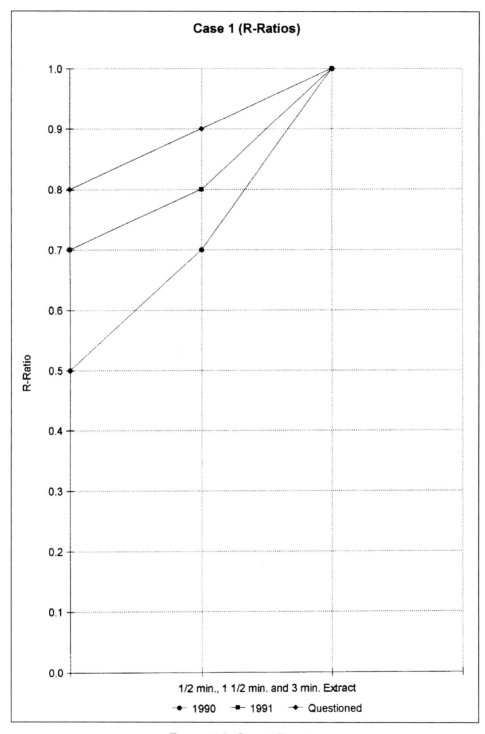

Figure 11.2. Case 1: R-ratios.

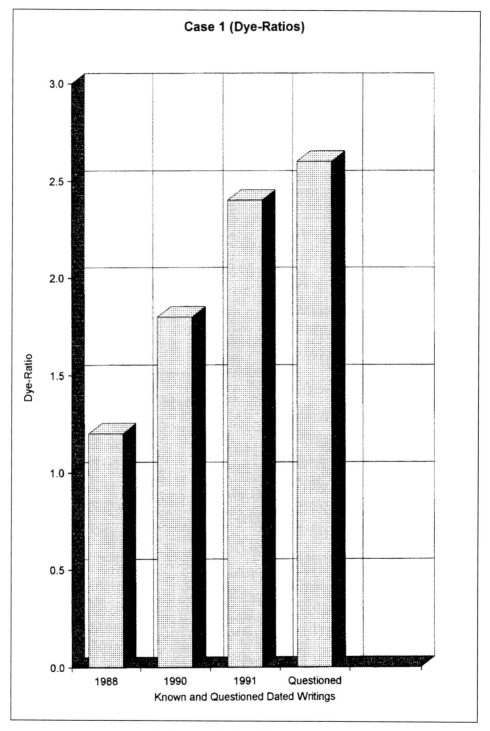

Figure 11.3. Case 1: Dye ratios.

CASE 2

This case involved a last will and testament and a codicil to this will. The will was dated 1982 and the codicil was dated 1988. Both were prepared on the same brand of white bond paper. Authentic signatures of the decedent were present on both the will and the codicil.

The question was whether handwritten changes to the codicil were made in 1988, when the decedent was still alive or were the changes made after his death by one of his sons in 1990. The son admitted the changes were in his handwriting and that the changes were favorable to him, but he said his father signed the codicil after the changes were made.

Examination of the ink used for the decedent signature and the handwritten changes to the codicil revealed that the same formulation of Bic black ballpoint ink was used for the signature and the changes on the codicil. The percent extraction test performed on both writings showed that there was a substantial difference between the relative dryness of the ink used for the signature and the changes to the codicil. This means that the signature and the changes could not have been made at the same time (see Figure 11.4). To determine whether the changes were made before or after the death of the decedent, an accelerated aging test was performed. Some inks extract more completely as the ink ages, whereas other inks extract less completely with age.

This Bic black ballpoint ink is known to extract more completely as the ink ages.

The accelerated aging test was performed as described in Chapter 8 and revealed that the heated signature ink extracted more completely than the unheated ink used for the changes. This means that the ink used for the changes to the codicil were added at a much later time than the signature of the decedent (see Figure 11.5). Faced with these laboratory findings, the son finally admitted he made the changes after his father died, but he still claimed his father wanted the changes to be made.

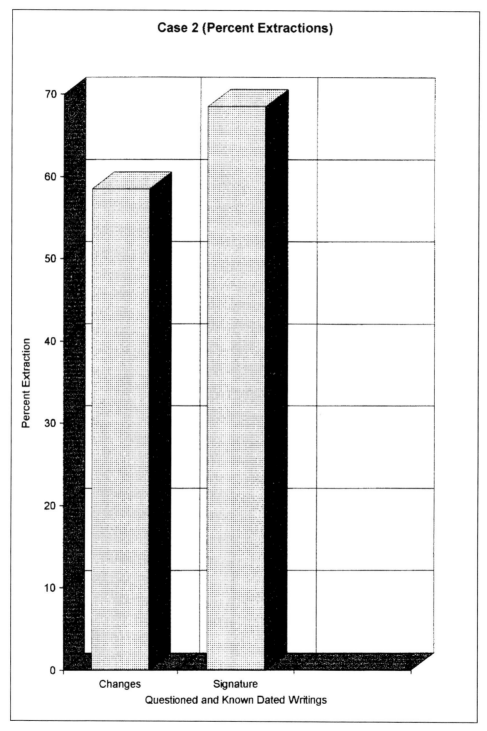

Figure 11.4. Case 2: Percent extractions.

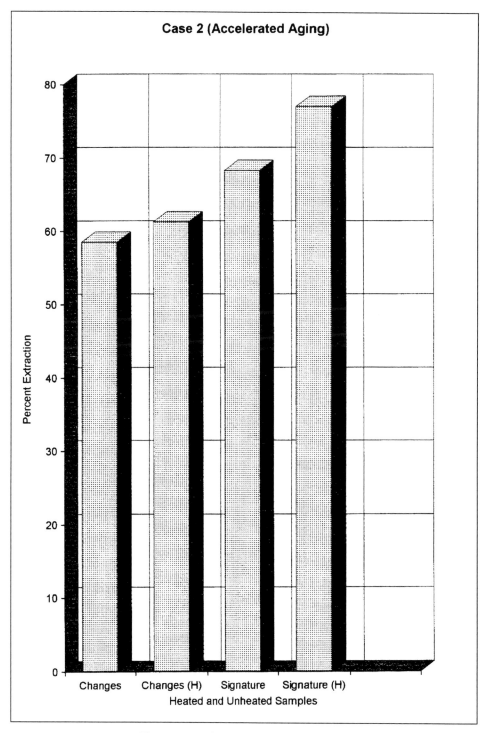

Figure 11.5. Case 2: Accelerated aging.

CASE 3

This case involved a divorce. The wife sued her husband for a divorce and at issue was the value of her husband's business. The husband operated a small business that he claimed had gone down in value over the previous 10 years prior to the lawsuit. As proof, he produced a document that showed declining profits over this 10-year time period of 1983 to 1993. The husband obviously wanted to reduce the amount of alimony he would have to pay. The divorce was filed in 1994 and the laboratory examination of the document was performed in 1995.

Examination of the inks used to prepare the document revealed three different inks were used. A Bic blue ballpoint ink was used for the years 1983, 1988, and 1993. A Papermate blue ballpoint ink was used for the years 1984, 1985, and 1991. A Bic black ballpoint ink was used for the four remaining years.

The author performed relative age comparison tests on the inks used for the oldest and most recent years for each type of ink. If the document was prepared contemporaneously, there should have been a gradual change in the dryness of the various inks used for the different years. However, the results of the examination revealed that the inks used for the oldest and newest entries each had the same level of dryness. The author concluded from these results that all of the entries over the 10-year time period were all written at the same time, some time in 1993–or more recently (see Figure 11.6). As with cases 1 and 2, the husband admitted he prepared the document in 1994, the year the divorce was filed. At this point, the husband claimed he rewrote the document to be more legible and the original notes were destroyed.

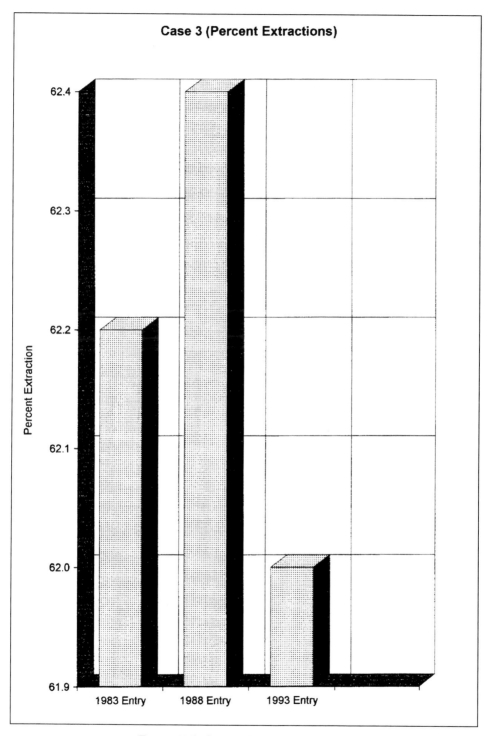

Figure 11.6. Case 3: Percent extractions.

CASE 4

This case involves alleged legal malpractice. A large law firm was accused of improperly handling the affairs of an extremely large manufacturing company. At issue were several large accounting spreadsheets showing sales figures. These spreadsheets were all initialed by various individuals and the question was whether the initials were placed on the spreadsheets contemporaneously with their purported dates over a period of eight years–or whether the initials were all written at the same time, after the lawsuit was filed in 1996. Other known dated writings on similar paper dated 1995 were also provided for examination. The spreadsheets were dated from 1987 to 1995 and the laboratory examination was performed in 1996. The author did this examination on behalf of the law firm, the defendants in the case.

Examination of the initials on the spreadsheets revealed they were all written with the same Mittenwald-Chemie black ballpoint ink formulation over the eight-year time period. Two known dated writings made in 1995 were also signed with this same ink. This provided a perfect situation for determining if the initials were all written at the same time and if the initials were written in 1995, instead of on their purported dates.

The percent extraction and dye ratio methods were used to compare the relative dryness of inks used for the initials and the inks from the known dating writings. As the law firm expected, all inks, questioned and known, had the same level of dryness, meaning the initials were all written in 1995, not contemporaneously as was claimed by the manufacturer (see Figures 11.7 and 11.8).

The author was required to testify in this case. Even though the jury believed his testimony, for other reasons, they found in favor of the plaintiff in the case.

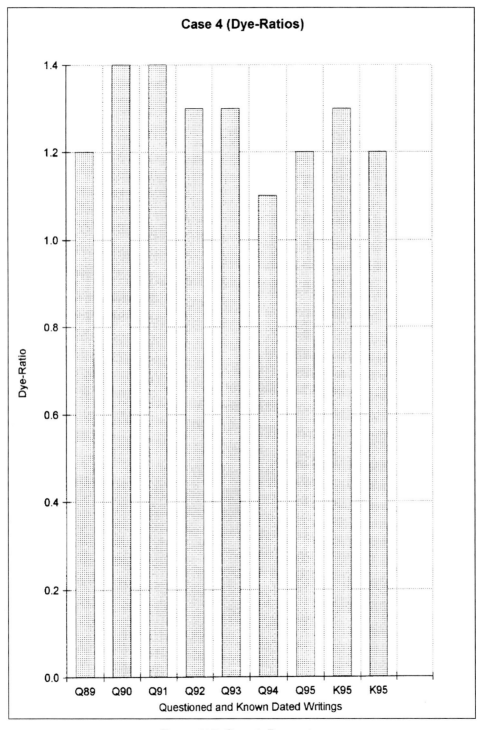

Figure 11.7. Case 4: Dye ratios.

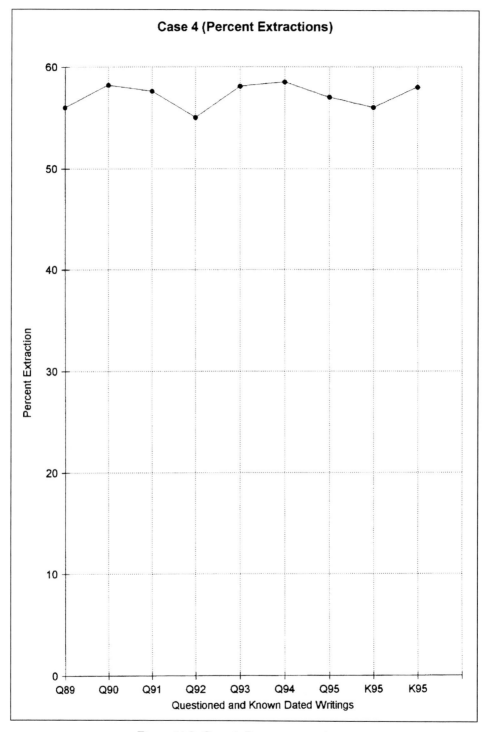

Figure 11.8. Case 4: Percent extractions.

CASE 5

This was an alleged wrongful termination case. The plaintiff was a lawyer who was fired by a large law firm for alleged deteriorating performance from 1988 to 1992. In their defense, the law firm produced five performance evaluations. Only the 1988 performance evaluation showed satisfactory performance. The other evaluations all indicated unsatisfactory performance. The plaintiff claimed that he only received the 1988 evaluation and that he was always told that he was doing a good job. The lawsuit was filed in 1992, and the laboratory examination of the five performance evaluations was also done in 1992.

Analysis of the various inks used to prepare the five performance evaluations revealed that two different inks were used. A Bic black ballpoint ink was used for the 1988, 1990, and 1992 evaluations. A Papermate blue ballpoint ink was used for the years 1989 and 1991. No known dated writings were available for comparison. Relative age comparisons of the matching inks were performed using the R-ratio and percent extraction methods.

The results of these examinations showed that the Bic black ballpoint inks used for the 1990 and 1992 performance evaluations had the same level of dryness, but these were substantially different from the dryness of the same ink on the 1988 evaluation. These findings were sufficient to conclude that the 1990 and 1992 evaluations were prepared at the same time in 1992, after the lawsuit was filed. The 1988 performance evaluation was most likely authentic.

The comparison of the dryness of the Papermate inks on the 1989 and 1991 performance evaluations showed that these inks also had the same level of dryness. Since a substantial difference in dryness of inks written two years apart would have been expected, these findings also lead to the conclusion that the 1989 and 1991 performance evaluations were written at the same time. Because there would be no logical reason for the law firm to prepare these two evaluations in 1991, it was concluded that these two evaluations were also prepared after the lawsuit was filed in 1992. (See Figures 11.9–11.12 for the results of the relative age comparison tests.) Testimony on this evidence was given at trial and the law firm was found guilty of wrongful termination and the plaintiff was awarded a large sum of money to compensate him for loss of income and his difficulty in finding new employment opportunities.

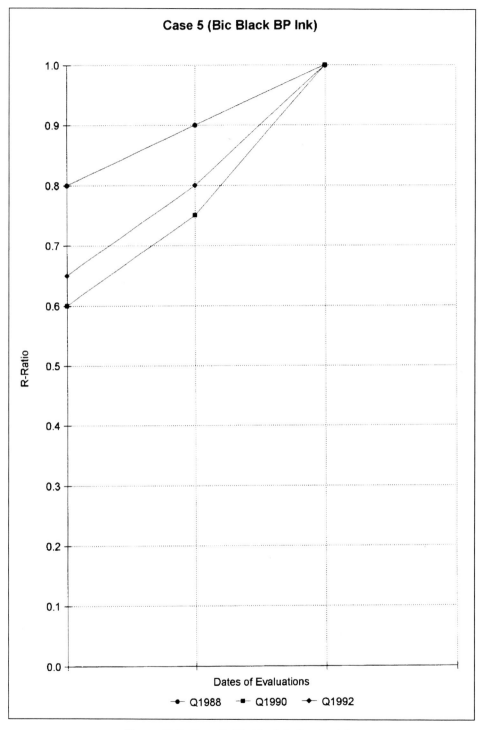

Figure 11.9. Case 5: Bic black ballpoint ink.

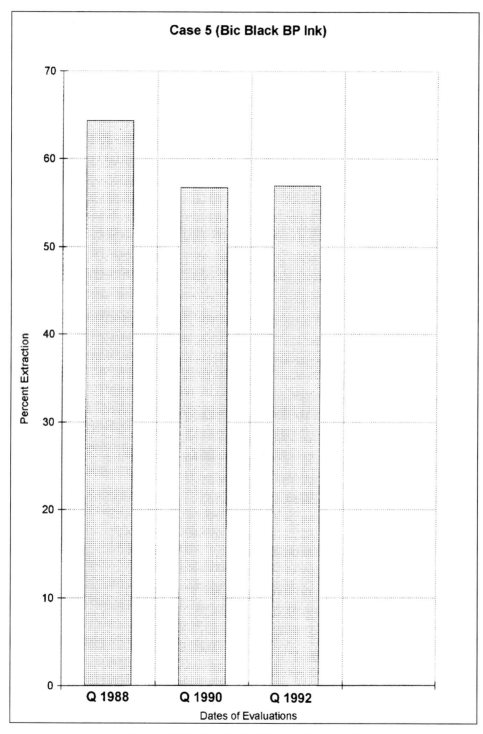

Figure 11.10. Case 5: Bic black ballpoint ink.

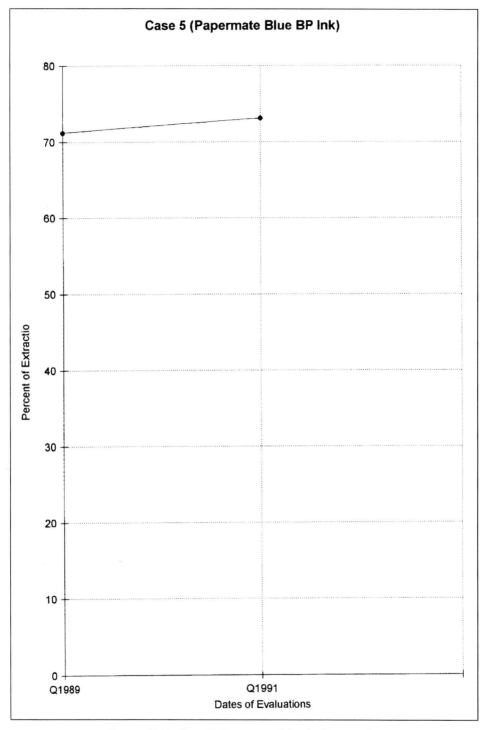

Figure 11.11. Case 5: Papermate blue ballpoint ink.

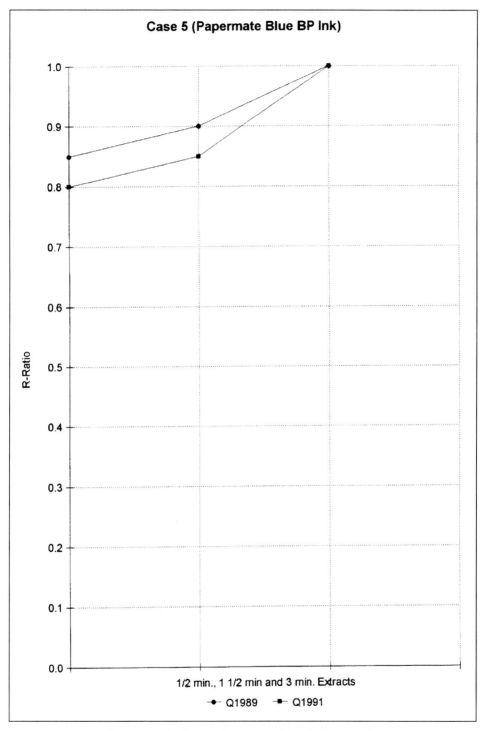

Figure 11.12. Case 5: Papermate blue ballpoint ink.

CASE 6

This case involved disputes between two different landowners involving billions of dollars. The dispute was over which of the two landowners had legal rights to certain properties. The plaintiff provided a ledger book that listed acquisitions of various properties from the defendant (the other land owner). The defendant claimed he never relinquished ownership of the properties. The entries in the ledger were dated from 1971 to 1990. The lawsuit was filed in 1991 and the defendant retained the author to examine the ledger in 1992.

Analysis of a random sampling of the inks used in the ledger revealed that only three different inks were used for the entire 19-year time period. The inks identified were a Bic black ballpoint, a Bic blue ballpoint and a different formula of another Bic black ballpoint ink made only in France.

Again relative age comparison tests were performed on the matching inks. This time the dye ratio method was used. A total of 15 entries in the record were analyzed. The results of this examination revealed that the matching inks used for the 15 entries all had the same dye ratios.

Since it has been scientifically established that ink dye ratios change with age, this was sufficient to conclude that all 15 entries tested over the 19-year time period had to be written at the same time—either after the lawsuit was filed in 1992 or shortly before. (See Figures 11.13, 11.14, and 11.15 for the results of the dye ratio tests.)

This case was settled during the author's cross-examination at trial. The evidence was overwhelming and the plaintiff's attorney was getting nowhere with his cross-examination.

REFERENCES

1. Brunelle, R.: Brunelle Forensic Laboratories.

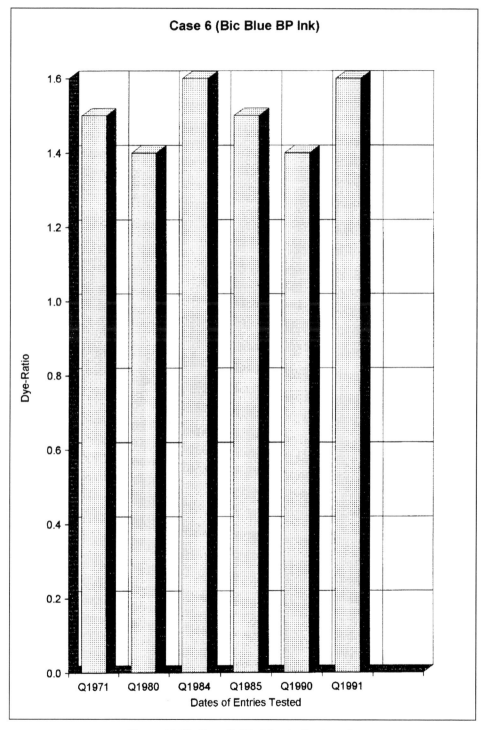

Figure 11.13. Case 6: Bic blue ballpoint ink.

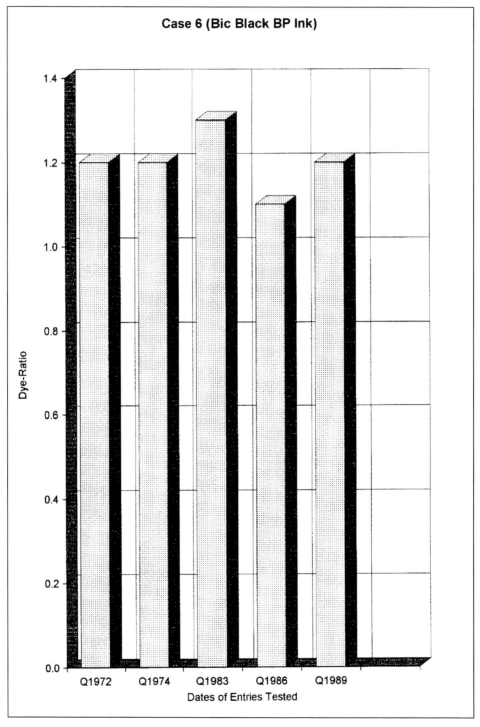

Figure 11.14. Case 6: Bic black ballpoint ink.

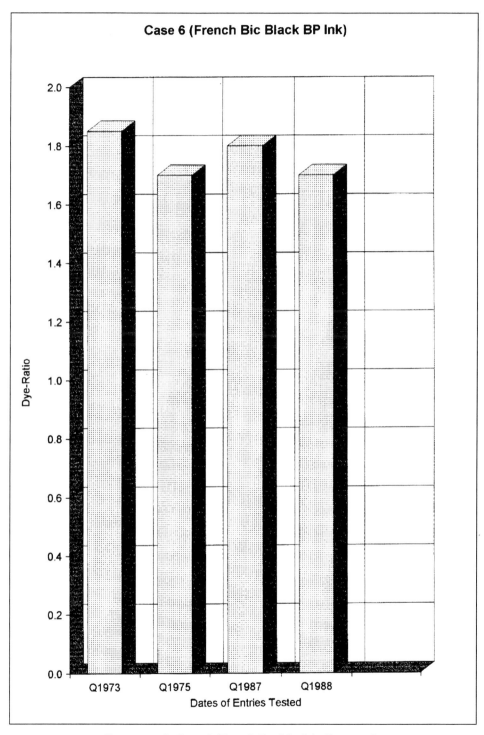

Figure 11.15. Case 6: French Bic black ballpoint ink.

Chapter 12

THE SOCIETY OF FORENSIC
INK ANALYSTS (SOFIA)

In August, 1997, SOFIA was incorporated in the state of Virginia. The purpose of this organization is to advance the science of the forensic comparison, identification, and dating of inks on questioned documents. It all began in 1996 at an American Academy of Forensic Sciences meeting in New York City. At this meeting, Richard Brunelle, Albert Lyter, and Erich Speckin (all private ink dating chemists) sat down in a hotel room to discuss and try to resolve some differences of opinions that existed among them. Everyone agreed that for the sake of the profession, ink analysts should use the same methods for relative age comparisons and that they needed to work together to establish criteria for reaching conclusions based on these techniques.

In July, 1997, the same people met again at Speckin Forensic Laboratories. At this meeting Robert Kuranz, another private examiner, was also present. At this meeting everyone agreed that a professional organization should be established to advance the science of forensic ink analysis and to set standards for chemists performing these examinations in connection with criminal and civil investigations. The organization was to be called the Society of Forensic Ink Analysts (SOFIA). At this meeting, these analysts made progress deciding which relative age comparison methods were acceptable and they designed studies to determine the effects of paper and ink thickness on these methods. Richard Brunelle was elected to be the first president of SOFIA for a two-year term. Also elected for two-year terms were Albert Lyter, Vice-President; Robert Kuranz, Secretary-Treasurer; and Erich Speckin was elected to the Board of Directors.

Neil Holland and Gus Lesnevich were named charter members.

After the July, 1997 meeting, Richard Brunelle wrote the bylaws and the requirements for membership in SOFIA and arranged for the incorporation of SOFIA in Virginia on August 17, 1997.

Richard Brunelle hosted the next meeting of SOFIA at Brunelle Forensic Laboratories in Fredericksburg, VA. At this meeting, SOFIA members, now including Kenneth Crawford of the state crime laboratory in Texas, agreed on several issues, including, the effects of paper, natural aging curves for inks, accelerated aging of inks, appropriate use of the dye ratio method, statistical criteria for determining whether inks are the same or different age, effects of ink thickness, linearity of densitometer measurements, and other matters.

At this meeting experiments were designed and later carried out by Richard Brunelle at Speckin Forensic Laboratories. SOFIA members studied the effects of storage conditions and the effects of paper on relative age comparison tests. Albert Lyter provided the ink samples for this research. The results of this research can be found in Chapter 10.

In just a few years, SOFIA has accomplished a great deal to establish uniform and acceptable methods for use in the relative age comparisons of ink. SOFIA members have conducted collaborative studies that have validated the R-ratio and percent extraction methods and the use of accelerated aging as a method for dating inks, when no standards are available for comparison with questioned inks. The creation of SOFIA has already lead to better understandings among the private examiners doing ink dating work, to the point where the only potential for disagreements lies in the interpretation of results. Differences of opinion no longer exist on methodology.

In the future, SOFIA members will conduct further methods validation studies and set standards for all ink dating chemists doing this type of work. Anyone interested in learning more about SOFIA can look at the SOFIA web site at: www.sofia-ink.org. This site has the SOFIA bylaws, membership requirements, the latest SOFIA news, meeting dates, accomplishments, and contact information.

Chapter 13

COURT ADMISSIBILITY OF RELATIVE AGE COMPARISON TECHNIQUES

A s mentioned earlier in this book, the admissibility of the relative age comparison techniques described in Chapter 8 have been routine since 1988, when ink dating chemists in the United States first began to widely use these methods.

Testimony concerning these techniques, by government chemists and chemists in the private sector, has been admitted over 1000 times in the United States, as well as in Hong Kong, Singapore, Israel, and Australia. Nevertheless, courts occasionally hold Frye or Daubert hearings in attempts to show that these methods are not reliable and/or have not been adequately evaluated.

In this chapter, we list the requirements of both Frye and Daubert for the admissibility of scientific evidence. We also describe courts' rulings at these hearings that challenged ink dating methodology. Then we cover the amendments to the Federal Rules of Evidence that went into effect in December, 2000.

DAVIS/FRYE RULE

To be admitted under Davis/Frye, a novel technique upon which an expert formed an opinion must have gained general scientific acceptance for reliability.[1] It is not necessary to establish infallibility if the results are reasonably certain.[2] The general acceptance for reliability must be established by disinterested and impartial experts.[3] Most judges will admit testimony based on novel techniques and leave it up to the jury to decide how much weight the testimony should be given.

In *United States v. Bonds,*[4] the Sixth Circuit made several pertinent observations about the Frye requirements:

- General acceptance exists when a substantial portion of the pertinent scientific community accepts the theory, principles, and methodology underlying scientific testimony, because they are grounded in valid scientific principles.
- Unanimity of scientific opinion is not required for general acceptance.
- Even the absence of support among a majority of the pertinent scientific community does not rule out general acceptance under Frye.
- The general acceptance test is designed solely to uncover whether there is a general agreement among scientists in the field that this scientific data is not based on a novel theory or procedure that is mere speculation or conjecture.
- Even substantial criticism about a theory or procedure is insufficient to demonstrate that the theory or procedure is not generally accepted.
- A particular procedure or theory will be not considered generally accepted only if: (1) it lacks acceptance of most of the pertinent scientific community, and (2) a substantial part of that community disfavors it.
- Whether a mistake was made in arriving at a conclusion is a jury question.
- Questions or disputes about scientific applications of a procedure or the accuracy of test results go to the testimony's weight, and do not render the theory or methodology invalid or not generally accepted.

Publication of a test or technique in recognized scientific journals which are peer reviewed is considered strong evidence of its scientific validity and general acceptance.[5] Unpublished studies, however, carry little weight.[6] All of the techniques described in Chapter 8 of this book for the dating of inks have been published in peer-reviewed journals. Furthermore, there are several ink chemists in the United States who have been using these techniques on a daily basis for over ten years.

Therefore, the question of whether ink dating is new and novel is really a moot point at this time.

DAUBERT RULE

The Daubert standard is considered to be more permissive than the Davis/Frye Rule. The case of *General Electric v. Joiner Daubert* held "that the austere Frye standard of general acceptance had not been carried over into the Federal Rules of Evidence"; allowing trial courts "to admit a somewhat broader range of scientific testimony than would have been admissible under Frye. . . ."[7]

In *Nelson v American Sterilizer Company* (this was not an ink case), the Michigan Court of Appeals originally reversed a trial court's exclusion of expert testimony, based in part on a determination that admissibility of the testimony of the experts must be determined under MRE 702.[8] The Court of Appeals then relied on Daubert to establish a standard for determining the evidential reliability or trustworthiness of the facts and data underlying the experts testimony under MRE 702 as follows: The court must determine whether the proposed testimony is derived from recognized scientific knowledge. To be derived from recognized scientific knowledge, the proposed testimony must contain inferences or assertions, the source of which rests in an application of scientific methods. Additionally, the inferences or assertions must be supported by appropriate objective and independent validation based on what is known, e.g. scientific and medical literature. This is not to say, however, that the subject of the scientific testimony must be known to a certainty. As long as the basic methodology and principles employed by an expert to reach a conclusion are sound and create a trustworthy foundation for the conclusion reached, the expert testimony is admissible no matter how novel.

COURT RULINGS ON INK DATING TESTIMONY

Since the inception of relative age comparison tests for dating inks on questioned documents, there have been only a few challenges under Davis/Frye or Daubert. In every case, the courts have ruled these tests were admissible. In *Schwochow v. Chung*[9] the appellate court found reversible error in the exclusion of Brunelle's expert testimony at trial and the case was remanded for a new trial. In *Hallum v. Reynolds-Marshall,*[10] Brunelle's work was unsuccessfully attacked as not being scientifically reliable or generally accepted in the scientific community. Brunelle had a few other Frye or Daubert hearings, but no rulings were made by the courts in these cases by the courts because all cases were settled during his cross-examination. After hearing Brunelle's testimony, insurance carriers did not want to risk letting the cases go to the juries.

In *Janopoulos v. Harvey L. Warner*,[11] a Daubert hearing was held to challenge ink dating work performed by Robert Kuranz. The challenge was unsuccessful. In fact the court even allowed another expert to testify to Kuranz' results and to use these results in reaching his own conclusions.

Erich Speckin's testimony has been challenged at least twice.[12,13] Both judges accepted Speckin's testimony, despite Davis/Frye challenges. These are the only challenges to ink dating testimony given by recognized experts of which the authors are aware.

AMENDMENTS TO FEDERAL RULES OF EVIDENCE[14]

In April, 2000, Supreme Court Chief Justice William H. Rehnquist submitted amendments to the Federal Rules of Evidence to Congress. Those new rules, which will affect expert testimony in federal courts in the United States, are listed below.

The Supreme Court of the United States Ordered:

1. That the Federal Rules of Evidence for the United States District Courts be, and they hereby are, amended by including therein amendments to Evidence Rules 103, 404, 701, 702, 703, 803(6), and 902
2. That the foregoing amendments to the Federal Rules of Evidence shall take effect on December 1, 2000, and shall govern all proceedings thereafter commenced and, insofar as just and practicable, all proceedings then pending.
3. That THE CHIEF JUSTICE be, and hereby is, authorized to transmit to the Congress the foregoing amendments to the Federal Rules of Evidence in accordance with the provisions of Section 2072 of Title 28, United States Code.

THE NEW RULES REGARDING EXPERT TESTIMONY
Rule 702. Testimony by Experts

If scientific, technical, or other specialized knowledge will assist the trier of fact to understand the evidence or to determine a fact in issue, a witness qualified as an expert by knowledge, skill, experience, training, or education, may testify thereto in the form of an opinion or otherwise, if (1) the testimony is based upon sufficient facts or data, (2) the testimony is the product of reliable principles and method, and (3) the witness has applied the principles and methods reliably to the facts of the case.

Rule 703. Bases of Opinion Testimony by Experts

The facts or data in the particular case upon which an expert bases an opinion or inference may be those perceived by or made known to the expert at or before the hearing. If of a type reasonably relied upon by experts in the particular field in forming opinions or inferences upon the subject, the facts or data need not be admissible in evidence in order for the opinion or inference to be admitted. Facts or data that are otherwise inadmissible shall not be disclosed to the jury by the proponent of the opinion or inference unless the court determines that their probative value in assisting the jury to evaluate the expert's opinion substantially outweighs their prejudicial effect.

REFERENCES

1. *People v. Young* (After Remand), 425 Mich 470, 473, 1986.
2. *People v. Lee,* 212 Mich App 228, 262, 1995.
3. *People v. Young,* supra, at 479, n 12.
4. *United States v. Bonds,* 12 F3d 540, 561–63 (CA 6, 1993).
5. *People v. Stoughton,* 185 Mich App 219, 226–29, 1990.
6. *People v. Young,* supra at 475–76.
7. *Nelson v. American Sterilizer Company* (On Remand), 223 Mich App 485, 1997.
8. Nelson, supra, at 453 Mich 946, 1996.
9. *Schwochow v. Chung,* 657 NE2d 312, 316–17 (Ohio App, 1995).
10. *Hallum v. Reynolds-Marshall,* Kennebec, ME Superior Court (Case No. CV-85-335 and CV-86-454, p. 47.
11. *Janopoulos v. Harvey L. Warner & Assoc,* 866 F Supp 1086, 1096–97 (ND, 1994)
12. In the Matter of Jose G. Higuera, MD (Department of Consumer & Industry Services, Docket No. 96-0616), 4/23/97, pp52–53, by Judge Renee A. Ozburn.
13. *People v. Higuera* (30th District Court Case No. 96-2740-FY), 10/28/97, pp. 145–53 by Judge L. Kim Hoagland.
14. Amendments to the Federal Rules of Evidence, U.S. Government Printing Office, Washington: 2000; 64–380.

Appendix

FORENSIC INK ANALYSIS RESOURCES

An abundance of information is now available on the World Wide Web; however, because website addresses can change, we have included a few in this text. The SOFIA website will maintain links to websites of scientific information and organizations with relevance to ink analysis.

General Information

Sofia: www.sofia-ink.org
FBI Forensic Science Communications Newsletter:
http://www.fbi.gov/programs/lab/fsc/current/index.htm

Writing Ink Manufacturers

Formulabs–529 Fourth Ave. Escondido, CA 92025
(In 2002, Formulabs sold ballpoint ink manufacturing to National Ink)

Chromex–19 Clay St., Brooklyn, NY 11222

Mittenwald-Chemie–Innsbrucker Strasse 35, D-8102, Mittenwald, West Germany

National Ink–1717 W. Magnolia Ave., El Cajon, CA 92020

Hartley–1987 Placentia Ave., Costa Mesa, CA 92020

Trade Associations

Writing Instrument Manufacturer's Association

INDEX

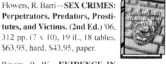
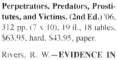

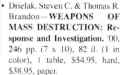